Miracles Happen

A Prayer Guide
For Desperate People

Carole Whang Schutter

───── ❖ ─────
Rhema House Publishing

Miracles Happen
Copywrite © 1999, by Carole Whang Schutter

All rights reserved. Written permission from the publisher is required prior to use or reproduction of any part of this book, except for brief quotations in critical reviews or articles.

Requests for information should be sent to:
RHEMA HOUSE PUBLISHING
P.O. Box 1067
Basalt, Colorado 81621-1067
www.miracleshappen.com

All scripture quotations, unless otherwise indicated, are taken from the HOLY BIBLE, NEW INTERNATIONAL VERSION®. NIV®. Copywrite© 1973, 1978, 1984 by International Bible Society. Used by permission of Zondervan Publishing House. All rights reserved.

Scripture quotations noted KJV are from The King James Version of the Holy Bible.

*This book is dedicated
to the Lord
who is my inspiration in all things.*

CONTENTS

Acknowledgements		7
Introduction		9
1.	Anything God, Just Help Me	13
2.	Faith Can Move Mountains	23
3.	Don't Quit—Praise, Praise, Praise	29
4.	Life is an Obstacle Course	35
5.	Do I have to forgive *Everyone?*	45
6.	The Kingdom Within	50
7.	Power in Numbers	60
8.	Give it to God	67
9.	Love is Not a Choice	71
10.	God Can Use Anyone	79
11.	Surrender	90
12.	Keys to the Kingdom	100

ACKNOWLEDGEMENTS

A special word of thanks to Pastor Dennis Leonard of Heritage Christian Center who's inspiring sermons helped me get through a very dark period in my life. Thanks to all my sisters and brothers in Christ: Colleen Nomura, Phyllis Ramia, Jerel and Sandy Miller, Lincoln Whang, Wanda and Lloyd Horibe and my mother, Nancy Shizue Whang, who never stopped believing in me.

INTRODUCTION
❖

A pastor once told me that you always know when God is talking to you because He always expects you to do things you either don't want to do or feel you can't do. However, when God calls your name—guess what? He's God and He will get your attention one way or another.

I always wanted to be a best-selling writer of novels. After my husband died, I threw myself into writing and produced some pretty good stuff. I received the most interesting rejections. Such as, *I don't think I'm capable of adequately representing this really great book. You have written a really fine novel, which you should be proud of. I'm sorry I don't have the time to represent it. Please send it somewhere else.*

Even after being signed by one of the top literary agents in the country, the rejections from the publishers kept coming. Finally my agent wrote, "This book deserves to be published. I can't understand why I can't sell it."

I can. It was God all along. He wanted to give me the desires of my heart, but first, He wanted me to write a book for Him. When it was first suggested to me that I write spiritual books I said, "I'm not qualified to write spiritual books. I never went to seminary or attended long-term Bible Studies. Maybe later. I promise."

That was not what God wanted to hear. He said NOW. And, as I said before, when God calls your name, He finds a way to make you listen.

I hike everyday in the Rocky Mountains during the late spring, summer and early fall. Hiking is not only good for the body and mind, but also for the soul, because I use this time to talk directly to God. After receiving another bizarre rejection, I went into the mountains and said, "Okay. I give up. What do you want me to write about?" The answer was prayer. "Lord," I argued, "there are so many books on prayer already. Besides, who am I to tell people how to pray?"

I felt as if the Lord told me, "Write a book about how miracles happen when you pray." My rebellious spirit thought, "That's a good one. My life is so messed up, I'm the last person to write a book on how miracles happen when you pray."

Oddly, as I began to throw up barriers, I began to see that my entire life was a testimony to the power of prayer. My life is ready to turn on a dime; I have no doubt that things will turn around miraculously. I speak by faith. If I were to walk by sight, I would give up. How comforting that troubles only last for the moment, but "joy comes in the morning".

This book is intended for desperate people who have reached the end of their rope and are willing to try anything. You may have already found that the doctors couldn't help, the psychics were wrong, the stars made you even more confused, crystals didn't pulsate in your hands and the shamans and kahunas told you things you didn't understand. Perhaps many of you were raised in Christian homes but felt like it missed the mark. You've tried every cure for your physical, emotional and spiritual ailments but have still come up empty.

If someone had told me fifteen years ago that I would

become a born again Christian, I would have thought they had gone crazy. I despised the religious fanaticism and condemnation that I saw in the Christianity I grew up with. During my quest to find myself, I studied, among other religions, Buddhism, Islam, Jehovah's Witness and Latter Day Saints. I had the honor of being kicked out of EST and Silva Mind Control for poisoning the would-be converts with my cynicism. I was told that I was incapable of making it.

It was only when I got into the Word at age 36 and began to examine the Bible for its historical accuracy and its prophecy that I began to understand the truth about Christianity. To my surprise, it wasn't about condemnation. The Bible says, "...there is now no condemnation for those who are in Christ Jesus" (Romans 8:1,NIV). True Christianity is about the power of love and the simple majesty of forgiveness that brings healing to our lives. This is the kingdom within that the Bible and pastors often talk about. It is the power of the Holy Spirit which enables us to do "all things in Christ Jesus that strengthens us" (Philippians 4:13,NIV). We have always had the power. We only need to learn how to tap into the power source by entering into the kingdom of God through Jesus Christ.

The gospel, or good news, of Jesus Christ is simple in comparison to organized religion. Interestingly, 'religion' is a Greek word meaning, 'to bind'. People mess up the simplicity of the gospel with rules so burdensome that Christians often resemble the Pharisees who condemned our Lord to the cross. The gospel of Jesus is that He loves us and forgives us all our sins through His sacrifice on the cross. Accept His love and enter into the circle of His love. This is where you will find the kingdom of God that has always been available to us through the indwelling of the Holy Spirit. We journey through life trying to find ourselves when the answer has always been right there within us.

The Holy Spirit, the Lord Jesus Christ and God the Father author this book. All honor and glory to the Holy Trinity. Thank you for the gifts and calling of God that are without repentance. Amen.

CHAPTER ONE

ANYTHING GOD, JUST HELP ME!

❖

How badly do you want or need a miracle? Do you need it enough to try anything? Do you want it so bad that you are willing to open your mind and your heart to receive all that God has in store for you?

Have you done all that you can and still feel hopeless and helpless? Do you feel that the only way out is for God to perform a miracle in your life? Then this book is for you. This book is for desperate people who no longer know what to do. It is not for those of you who still want to try it your way or man's way. Because God's way is about giving up control. God demands complete and total surrender. If you can't do that, close this book and go ahead and do it your way. But if you are so desperate that you can truly say, "Anything, God. Just help me," then you are ready to receive your miracle.

God is the God of last resorts. If you are reading this book, you are firmly implanted in the land of last resorts. It's okay. God reaches you in the valleys of your life and not the peaks. It's a principle of salvation for most people so don't feel bad about it. A friend of mine who recently went through some devastating times told me, "I feel bad because I only reach out to God when my life is falling apart. I can't help but feel that God's mad at me for that. I act as if I don't need Him when everything's good."

Unwittingly, my friend found the key to one of the most quoted passages in the Bible: "It is harder for a rich man to go to heaven than for a camel to go through the eye of a needle" (Matthew 19:23,24,NIV). A lot of rich people don't feel that they need God. May I add that you can be rich intrinsically as well as physically? Not all riches are counted in terms of wealth. Those who are so blessed also wonder why they need God. After all, they did it all themselves because they're so smart, so wonderful, such good people, etc. that they have never needed God. Why give God the credit for their peachy keen lives when they can take all the credit for themselves?

It is the biggest lie of the devil. Consider yourself blessed to have a "thorn in your flesh" that draws you close to the Lord (2 Corinthians 12:7,NIV). These are the blessings in the heartache. God loves you so much He is allowing you to go through these things so that you find Him before it's too late. It's your eternal life He's worried about. This life here on earth is just a passing breeze.

Try to imagine eternity. The vastness of space is representative of eternity, there is no beginning and there is no end. What is sixty or a hundred years on earth compared to that? If you don't believe in God and you don't believe in the ever after, no problem. Throw this book away and live your life as passionately as you can because, after all, life is short, you might as well enjoy it to the hilt.

However, if something in your soul tells you that there is a 1% chance that there might be something after death, don't you owe it to yourself to find out if it's true? Are you worth so little and is eternity so valueless that you refuse to spend any time examining Christianity and other religions of the world until you are convinced of the veracity of one of them? Do not reject Christianity without studying it. You hurt no one but yourself by doing so. With eternity on the line, do you really have no time to find out if whether everything the Bible says is true? You cannot take anyone else's word for it; this is something you have to do by yourself.

A word of condolence for the rich. Read the rest of Matthew 19:23-26 (NIV) regarding how difficult it is for the rich to get to heaven. After Jesus makes His famous statement, his disciples "were greatly astonished and asked, 'Who, then can be saved?' Jesus looked at them and said, 'with man this is impossible, but with God all things are possible.'" It's no big thing for God to make a camel walk through the eye of the needle. There is nothing that is too big for God. Keep that in your heart and confess it at every opportunity. "God can and will cure me of cancer. God can and will deliver my daughter from schizophrenia. Thank you for the healing." Announce in faith, "My son is on drugs and wants nothing to do with the Lord but by faith, I believe he will be delivered from substance abuse and worship the Lord Jesus Christ."

However, a lot of us don't really know what we want and some of us think we know what we want but we're not sure. We pray, "Please God, give me what I want. But only if that's what you want." We pray double-minded prayers because in truth, we're confused. We think we want something but doubt lingers in the back of our minds.

Admit to yourself, do you really know what you want? Honesty and surrender to the will of God are imperative to your success. You must be willing to surrender everything, even your entire world of minor feelings to Him. Don't hold anything back.

God cannot help you if you don't let Him. We pray, but we want control over our lives. We are unable to let go of our fears because we have become so accustomed to our insecurities and problems that we have actually become comfortable with them. The truth is that we often love our sins and are used to our problems. Our problems and sins stand in the way of the solution itself. We are afraid to elevate ourselves to a new level. We are afraid of becoming something we are not; living in fear that we will not be able to live in our 'new bodies' and in a 'New World. Be adventurous. Try letting go and seeing where God's mercy and grace takes you.

Pray and meditate on the thing you desire "without ceasing," making sure that it is not inconsistent with the Word of God. The Bible explains, "This is the confidence we have in approaching God: that if we ask anything according to His will, He hears us. And if we know that He hears us-whatever we ask-we know that we have what we asked of Him" (1John 5:14,NIV).

The ancient Babylonians had a saying, "When the gods want to punish you, they answer your prayers." Thank goodness our God is not a fickle, arbitrary God driven by humanlike emotions. However, its still important to make sure your desire is from God as desire driven wholly by your flesh could harm you.

King David wrote, "Delight yourself in the Lord and He will give you the desires of your heart" (Psalm 37:4,NIV). The word used for 'delight' in the Hebrew meant contentment and joy. Contentment in stressful, tragic situations only comes when we are able to surrender to God. We are discontent when we feel out of control of our lives and worry about the outcome of any situation. As we surrender everything to God, He begins to do a mighty work in our lives. He gives us the peace and joy that comes from knowing that He is in control and nothing is going to happen that is out of His will.

Through prayer and meditation on the word of God, I came to understand that it is God who puts desires into our hearts. If we surrender our will to Him, He begins to change us until our desires are consistent with His will. He eliminates those desires that would harm us or do not fit into His wonderful plan for our lives and give us new desires. We truly become 'new creations in Christ' as our hearts and our minds undergo a transformation. In this way, we begin to want what He wants for us.

After you have put your desires through the test, cover them symbolically with the blood of Jesus in prayer. Why do Christians 'plead the blood of Jesus' in their prayers? Jesus was the sacrificial, perfect Lamb of God. In accordance with God's command, the ancient Israelites took a perfect, unblemished lamb and sacrificed it for their sins. The blood was then applied to the earlobes, forehead, hands and feet of the priest to symbolize that every action, deed and thought was covered under the blood.

Before the Israelites were set free from Egypt, God commanded Moses to have the blood of an innocent lamb put over the lintel of each Jewish household so that the angel of death would 'pass over' their homes without slaying the firstborn of the household.

Life is in the blood. Without blood there is no life. Without blood, there is no forgiveness. The blood of Jesus thus symbolizes the washing away of sin in our lives. Because of this ability to cleanse, there is power in the blood.

We confess the blood of Jesus to invoke the power inherent within the life of Jesus Christ.

After symbolically covering your desires in the blood of Jesus, meditate on God's will. When you know that you know that this is what God wants for you and not simply what your flesh wants, receive it by thanking God for granting your wish before it materializes. This is a prayer of affirmation and faith.

Some of you may not even be Christians. In fact, I hope you're not all Christians because it is my desire to reach those who seek the God they do not know—in order to bring clarity and peace into their lives.

Now for those of you who are 'unchurched', let me give you a simple course in 'Christianese'. The Word is the Bible. Jesus is also referred to as the Word. The Holy Spirit is part of the Holy Trinity comprised of God the Father, God the Son and God the Holy Spirit. When Jesus left this earth to return to the Father after His resurrection from the cross, commonly celebrated as Easter, He left the Holy Spirit on earth to act as our intercessor before God the Father and to help us get by on this earth. This awesome time was called Pentecost. The Holy Spirit often prays through us and for us, especially when we are so broken, words will not (or cannot) even come out of our mouths. The indwelling of the Holy Spirit is what gives our prayer's power and direction. More on that later.

If you want or need a miracle in your life, you are living in the right century. Many theologians believe we are living in what has been euphemistically called the 'end times' or 'last days' when the second coming of Christ will usher in a new heaven and a new earth. Prior to Christ's return, the earth will undergo cataclysmic changes. In preparation for these 'end times,' God is harvesting souls.

God knows our human weakness demands proof of His existence. Being pragmatic and scientific, we can't or won't believe until we are given something tangible. God has always been in the miracle making business. Miracles are for today, not just yesterday. We have only to tap into His power.

It seems so simple, but it isn't. Not everyone gets a miracle. On the other hand, not everyone needs a miracle in order to believe. God blesses those who have not seen and yet believe. God supplies His miracles according to His grace and His mercy. However, there are things we can do to petition God to work a miracle on our behalf.

First of all, I don't mean to offend anyone, but Jesus says, "I am the way, the truth and the light. NO MAN comes before the Father, except through me" (John 14:6,NIV). When He said that no man comes before God except through the intercession of Jesus Christ, He meant it. Mary and Joseph can't intercede. Neither can Buddha or Mohammed. No one can intercede and be heard except the Lord Jesus Christ and the Holy Spirit. All of these people may have been wonderful people, but they cannot intercede for you to the Almighty God. If you want what no one but God can give you, you have to tap into the power source. You have to go to the main man, Jesus, who died on the cross for your sins.

Now this may be the first major stumbling block for some of you. You may even be agnostic or atheist. My own son said to me, "How can I pray for Jesus to help me when I don't even really believe in Him?"

General Lew Wallace, the author of Ben Hur read the

Bible in order to prove that it was not the word of God. Instead, he became a devout Christian. There have been many other examples of men who did the same thing. If you don't believe, I challenge you to read the Bible. I am positive that even with the wrong attitude and a heavy dose of cynicism, if you study God's word, your life will be transformed. If you don't believe in God and/or Jesus, your first step toward a miracle is to start reading the Bible.

Jesus is quoted as saying, "Ask and it will be given to you, seek and you will find, knock and the door will be opened unto you" (Matthew 7:7,NIV). God never says anything He doesn't mean. Ask God to reveal Himself to you. God loves honesty above everything else. He knows that many of you simply believe in a higher being whose name you're not sure of. God is a generic enough name to use if that's all you can bring yourself to say. Pray to Him, "God, I don't know who you are or if you're even real. But I want to know. I'm desperate. No one can help me; I'm seeking you. In obedience I will pray in Jesus' name, even if I don't really believe. What I do believe is that you will make Jesus real to me. Help me to find you God."

God will never let you down with a sincere prayer like this. What He hates is lying. You can get through this first step of praying in Jesus' name while you seek God. Keep this in mind. The Lord Jesus Christ said, "I tell you the truth, my Father will give you whatever you ask in my name…Ask and you will receive, and your joy will be complete" (John 16:23,NIV).

Is there anything too hard for God? On the other hand, is there anything too trivial or too small for God? The Word says that God knows when the sparrow falls out of the tree; don't you think that you're worth more than a sparrow? (Matthew 10:29,30,NIV).

A Real Estate Developer in Aspen, once chided me, "You're not supposed to bother God with small requests. You're supposed to only go to Him for the big stuff."

I asked, "Where in the Bible does it say that?"

He replied, "I don't know, but my minister told me that."

I'm sorry to differ with his minister, but I told Him that it was my understanding from reading the Word that God wanted to be involved with every aspect of our lives. The apostle Paul says, "Pray in the Spirit on all occasions with all kinds of prayers and requests" (Ephesians 6:18,NIV). Everything is to be brought to the throne. "Do not be anxious about anything, but in everything, by prayer and petition, with thanksgiving, present your requests to God. And the peace of God, which transcends all understanding, will guard your hearts and your minds in Christ Jesus" (Philippians 4:6,7,NIV).

Praying about everything is the manifestation of obedience and surrender to the Lord God Almighty. So I told this very successful Real Estate Developer, "I even pray about parking spaces."

A year later the developer came to me and said, "I've thought a lot about what you've said. I think you're right. As a matter of fact, my minister has changed his mind and believes more like you. However, I still haven't gotten around to asking Him for parking spaces."

There are numerous verses in the Bible regarding prayer that I will share with you throughout the course of this book. They are imperative to victory and essential to the miracle.

CHAPTER TWO

FAITH CAN MOVE MOUNTAINS
───────── ❖ ─────────

Some of the most powerful verses in the Bible regarding prayer can be found in the book of Mark 11:22-25,NIV. Jesus tells the apostles, "Have faith in God. I tell you the truth, if anyone says to this mountain, 'Go, throw yourself into the sea,' and does not doubt in his heart but believes that what he says will happen, it will be done for him. Therefore I tell you, whatever you ask for in prayer, believe that you have received it, and it will be yours. And when you stand praying, if you hold anything against anyone, forgive him, so that your Father in heaven may forgive you your sins."

Powerful stuff. Let's examine the truths in this passage individually.

"Have faith in God." How great is your faith? Do you believe that God is all powerful, almighty, omniscient and omnipotent? Do you believe that He can do anything? Do you believe that He is the master of the Universe and that He is in control?

When a desperate father came to see Jesus about healing his son, Jesus asked him this simple question. "Do you believe that I can do this?" The father cried out, "I do believe, help me with my unbelief" (Mark 9:14-32,NIV). Jesus healed his son. It's okay to say that to the Lord. We may believe, but not with all our hearts and all our minds. Ask God to help you with your unbelief. And for those of you who don't believe; pray, seek God, read the Bible, go to church, find someone in that church to mentor you and God will reward you by giving you the faith and belief that you need. I promise. More importantly, the Bible promises. Ask, seek, knock and you will find. Furthermore, Jesus said if you had "faith as small as a mustard seed, you can say to this mountain, 'Move from here to there' and it will be moved. Nothing will be impossible for you" (Matthew 17:20,NIV).

Remember that even Jesus could not do miracles in His hometown of Nazareth because of the unbelief of the townspeople. You tie God's hands with your unbelief. Believe in the God who believes in you and is calling your name right now or you would not be reading this book.

"Whatever you ask for in prayer, believe that you have received it and it will be yours" (Jesus, as quoted in Mark 11:24,NIV). This is the power of positive thinking. Believe that you have received. Do not doubt in your mind the power of God to give you whatever it is you want. Do not doubt the depth and breadth of God's love for you. James 1:6-8(NIV) in the Bible says, "But when he asks, he must believe and not doubt, because he who doubts is like a wave of the sea, blown and tossed by the wind. That man should not think he will receive anything from the Lord; he is a double-minded man, unstable in all he does."

Jesus said that God is our Father and if we hunger, He will not give us stones to eat, but bread (Matthew 7:9,NIV). God is not a mean, punishing God. He is a God of grace, mercy and goodness. There is no beginning and no end to His love. He loves us and wants us to be happy. Believe with all your heart that He wants to answer your prayers and in fact, has already done so. Wait for the manifestation of the answer to your prayers.

FAITH CAN MOVE MOUNTAINS

A beautiful African-American doctor felt that God wanted her to volunteer her time to a famous healing evangelist's ministry. This young doctor was just starting out her career and faced a mountain of debt because of student loans. The doctor also wanted to find someone to marry. The last thing she wanted to do was spend her own money and a lot of her time in ministry at this particular moment in her life. However, God wouldn't give up until she finally stepped out in faith and obeyed.

Whenever God calls your name, it will cost you something. Whether it's a financial loss or the loss of a relationship, there always seems to be a price we have to pay. I believe it's because God wants to see how faithful you are. He wants to know where your priorities lie.

The young doctor ignored common sense and decided to serve God, no matter how hard it was going to be. In faith, she continued to pray to God for help in her finances and for a Christian husband. God told her to buy a wedding dress because He was bringing her a husband soon. At the time, she couldn't afford a wedding dress, but she bought it anyway, so convinced was she that God was in the process of answering her prayers. She was walking by faith and not by sight. Soon after, the Lord brought her a husband who she met through the evangelist's ministry. He was a world famous athlete who happened to be very, very rich. Despite her circumstances, the doctor had stepped out in faith and believed God for her miracle. Imagine if she had denied God's promises and refused to listen to His direction. Sometimes you don't know why God tells you to do the things He does. Just remember that He has a perfect plan for your life.

"Now faith is being sure of what we hope for and certain of what we do not see" (Hebrews 11:1,NIV). Be positive. Walk by faith and not by sight. Say to the mountains, the trees, the sky, and your friends and family, "by faith I receive my miracle." Thank the Lord every day for answering your prayers. "Thank you Lord for my healing. By your stripes (the whip marks on the Lord Jesus Christ's back) I am healed." Speak it in faith. Believe it. This is faith by affirmation. Faith becomes pro-active at this point. Christians often call this 'stepping out in faith'.

In the movie, Indiana Jones and the Temple of Doom, Indiana looks out at a bottomless chasm and knows that the only way to his salvation is to take a step of faith into what looks like an abyss. He closes his eyes and steps out only to find that the abyss is an illusion, there is solid footing right beneath him. Sometimes we have to step out in faith where it looks the scariest and say, "I believe, help me with my unbelief. I am walking by faith and not by sight. I will step out because the Lord is going to catch me." Have no fear; God will be there. No matter how grim your situation, affirm your belief that God will do all He promises by saying, "Thank you Lord for my miracle." The more you say it, the more you will believe what you say. The more you believe, the more you will act as if your miracle is a done deal.

With God all things are possible. God can even change other people without their knowledge. He "hardened Pharaoh's heart" (Exodus 10:20,NIV) so that His miracles could be manifested in freeing the Israelites from Egypt.

I once faced a situation in court where my lawyer informed me that the judge had "already made up his mind." The judge was known for writing his decisions before entering the courtroom, and then sticking by them. The day before, my lawyer and the opposing counsel had a conference call with the judge to inform him that both sides had come to an agreement of sorts. He not only made clear his opposition to the agreement; he made clear his opposition to me.

My lawyer was stunned that I wasn't angry. He told me I had every right to be mad and that he thought the entire situation was outrageous. He asked me, "Why aren't you mad?"

I calmly told him, "Because the judge thinks he's in control, but he's not. I've given this entire case to God. It doesn't matter what the judge wants; God will put the words in his mouth even as he opens it to speak. He may even find himself contradicting himself. But however it ends up, its in God's hands and I will accept the final decision."

Leaving it in God's hands meant I called my prayer partners and asked them to pray for me. I even had my housekeeper and her prayer partner come and sit outside the courthouse and pray during the hearing. I covered the entire situation in prayer every way I could. I praised God for the judge and for the difficulty of my situation. I praised both sets of lawyers and the "thorn in my flesh" (2 Corinthians 12:7,NIV). I thanked God for this particular judge and his 'hard heart'. The bigger the obstacle, I knew, the greater the miracle.

The important thing to remember is that it's not enough to say the matter is in God's hands. Your job is to cover the situation with as much prayer as possible from yourself and others. That, and praising Him in every circumstance.

The next day the judge saw both lawyers in chambers

before the hearing. According to my lawyer, the judge first began to re-state his position when he suddenly changed his mind. When he came into the courtroom, his entire demeanor had softened and he startled the entire courtroom with his speech. One observer said, "I have never seen that particular judge change his mind before."

My lawyer later told me, "I don't believe it."

I smiled and said. "I told you God's in control."

Believe with all your heart that He is in control and wants to help.

That brings me to the importance of prayer groups and prayer partners. I called upon my prayer partners and even had some of them right there with me at the courthouse. There is power in numbers.

Our God is the God of the impossible. Believing and acting in faith are crucial to your miracle.

CHAPTER THREE

DON'T QUIT—PRAISE, PRAISE, PRAISE

❖

Don't ever give up. Praise the Lord, Praise Jesus and Praise the Holy Spirit constantly and consistently.

Prayer must be regular. A simple concept that is sometimes difficult to implement in our busy world. Set aside a prayer time and do it consistently. Jesus once gave an example of a woman who constantly bothered a judge with her pleas. In exasperation, the judge gave her what she wanted because she wouldn't give up. If we go before the throne of God with great persistence, He will answer our prayers. So many times, people give up just before their miracle. Don't. Keep knocking on that door. Pray without ceasing and the Lord will bless you for it.

God wants to know how much we want something and how far we will go to get it. Will our faith stand up if we don't immediately get our way or will we be like the Israelites and murmur against God when things don't go our way immediately? The Israelites had to wander in the wilderness for forty years because their complaining showed a lack of faith. You would think that anyone who saw the Red Sea parted would have tremendous faith in God. Instead, they feared the giants in the Promised Land and their ability to take that land. They forgot what the Lord had done for them in Egypt was "not by might, nor by power, but by my spirit" (Zechariah 4:6,NIV). Therein lay their victory.

Don't let unbelief and murmuring stop you from entering your Promised Land.

If you can remember that the fight is fixed because "the battle is not yours, but God's" (2 Chronicles 20:15,NIV), then you will not be afraid but able to rest in the assurance that God is on your side and you have nothing to worry about. Jesus tells you to give Him all your burdens. Put your problems on the altar and no matter what comes against you, believe "all things work for the good for those who love the Lord and are called according to His purpose" (Romans 8:28,NIV). After all, this is God's promise, so what are you worried about? Your job is simply to pray daily in all circumstances and praise the name of the Lord.

One of the most important aspects of prayer is that God lives in the praises of His people. Whenever any of God's people had a vision of heaven in the Bible, they saw the angels and the saints praising God and glorifying Him. There is power in praise. Praise unleashes the power of the Lord to work in your life. He is our King and worthy to be praised. He made us and watched over us even when we walked in darkness. He is the God who can do anything. Praise Him no matter what.

When I began to praise God for the misfortunes in my life, He began to show me the broader picture. He began to show me the how and the why of things. When I praised Him for having a million dollars worth of jewelry and gold stolen from me, He showed me that I had put my trust and my values in the 'things of the world'. With the loss, I had been set free from 'things'. I discovered that loss was nothing compared to losing the husband I loved to what was ruled as suicide. There is no value in things; losing all that made me realize my real riches were in heaven and that if the financial depression I feared really hit, God would take care of me. I stopped worrying about how I would survive a depression and found great peace in trusting the Lord for everything.

My husband's death was the hardest thing for me to praise God for. I did it out of obedience. God knew I was speaking it out of my mouth without feeling the words. In His mercy, God began to show me things that brought me tremendous peace. But the real miracle was that I stopped being mad at God for 'what He did to me'. I turned away from my bitterness and anger at God for not stopping my husband's death. After all, I believed with all my heart that God could do anything, so why didn't He stop it? I had the audacity to say to the King of Kings, "Thanks a lot, God. You finally gave me what I searched for all my life and then you took it away from me after eight and a half short years!"

Time and God's gentle touch have shown me how wrong I was. Who am I to doubt God? I now thank God for those eight and a half years. I thank God that I was able to feel such passion and love given and returned. I thank God that He made me so wonderfully that I have the capacity to love with every molecule of my being. I loved and was loved in the way people search for all their lives and sometimes never find. How lucky I was to have had what I had. And, no matter where God leads me from here on, I will praise Him for my life, just as it is, no complaints.

My manicurist in Aspen, Naoma, told me that when her sister was a of only two years old, she suffered third degree burns all over her body from a freak accident. Sometime after, Naoma's mother took her little girl to church, but unable to walk, she sat limply in her stroller. Then her mother did something truly remarkable. She got up and began thanking God and praising Him for keeping her child alive. In the midst of doing that, Naoma's sister suddenly jumped out of her stroller and began to run around the church. There wasn't a dry eye in the church.

Father knows best. Keep that in mind. He really does. Some of the worst things that ever happened to me turned out to be the best things for me. I know how difficult it is to praise God sometimes. One of my favorite Christian songs goes, "I offer Him the sacrifice of praise". It's a sacrifice to praise God when our life is falling apart. Do it anyway. The sacrifice of praise is the finest gift you can offer our King. Praising God, a friend of mine once told me, takes the focus off you and puts the focus on God.

It is important that you look at God as the source of all good things in life. God did not bring you sickness or take away your spouse. God is perfect goodness and grace. He has a wonderful plan in your life and in the lives of all your loved ones.

When my sons were living like the devil and getting into trouble constantly, I said, "I praise you God for my sons, just as they are." I realized that people have their own walk. Thank God I can stand on Acts 16:31(NIV): "Believe in the Lord Jesus Christ and you and your household will be saved." God pulls them into the flock in His own way and in His own time. Our role is to stand and trust Him, no matter what.

Praise is sweet incense to the Lord. When you praise Him, you stop your murmuring and complaining and He will stop to really listen to you. Faith and praise go together. They flow from the spirit and light the lamps in our life.

The fourth chapter in the book of Zechariah describes a solid gold lamp stand that the Lord told Zechariah was His Spirit. There were two olive trees, one to the right and one to the left of the lamp stand that poured out golden oil into two gold pipes. The Lord said, "These are the two who are anointed to serve the Lord of all the earth" (Zechariah 4:14,NIV). The two are sometimes referred to as faith and praise lighting the Spirit who makes all things possible. Thus, they are the main ingredients to the miracle because everything else follows.

Always start your prayer by praising God. I cannot overemphasize how important that is. Praise puts you in an attitude of worship and sets you up for meaningful prayer. Praise anoints you with the spirit of the Lord and enables you to pray in accordance to His will. It is therefore crucial in your prayers.

When you praise Him, acknowledge what He has done for you and tell Him how wonderful He is. Sometimes when I'm feeling down, I begin to praise and thank the Lord for everything and anything. I thank Him for the blue sky, for the mountains, for a lovely home to live in, for all the people that love me and after awhile I begin to wonder why I'm feeling so blue. I begin to realize how much I have and I begin to wonder what I'm complaining about. Such is the power of praise and the power of the spoken word. You are what you speak. Be careful about speaking negativity in your life lest you curse yourself with it. Jesus said, "For by your words you will be acquitted, and by your words you will be condemned" (Matthew 12:37,NIV).

Not only should you praise God, you should thank Him before you receive your answer. This is key, you must always thank God for answering your prayers even though the problem still exists. You must believe that He heard it in heaven and is already acting upon it. Believe that you have already received your miracle, even when your life seems even more messed up. As a matter of fact, when your life has really been turned upside down, it's usually a sign that your miracle is right around the corner.

CHAPTER FOUR

LIFE IS AN OBSTACLE COURSE, JUMP OVER!

❖

What happens when you pray and pray without ceasing and instead of things getting better, everything goes to hell in a hand basket? Well, it means that the devil is running scared because he can't stand it when you pray and praise the Lord God so he throws roadblocks along the way.

Our lives are like obstacle courses. As we race along life's path, there are many obstacles we must jump over or figure out a way to go around. Just as obstacles strengthen an athlete, we are strengthened each time we are forced to leap in the air and clear that obstacle. There are times we fall headfirst into the barrier but that shouldn't stop us.

I am reminded of the female candidate who could not scale the wall in the movie An Officer and a Gentleman. There came a time when she wanted to give up, but Richard Gere's character talked her into trying just a little bit more. When she finally scaled the wall, the smile of pride on her face was luminous. That was how I felt the first time I skied a black diamond run. I was so pleased with myself for skiing a run considered difficult. I felt a sense of accomplishment. I had scaled my mountain.

When troubles come our way, we should praise God that we have another opportunity to prove our faith, strengthen our walk and learn something we didn't know about the Lord and ourselves. Instead of complaining, we should delight in the fact that every obstacle is making our spirit muscles grow stronger. Whenever I'm feeling depressed about my problems, I confess the Biblical truth that God will not give me anything more than I can bear. Of course, I must admit that I've sometimes told God, "In case you don't know it, this is it. Or maybe you think I'm a lot tougher than I think I am." Then I sigh and remember that the Lord promised to "never leave me or forsake me" (Deuteronomy 31:6,NIV).

Praise God, there are blessings in problems. We are blessed in that we learn more from our setbacks than we do from our victories. We are blessed because each setback sets us up for an even greater victory. Most of all, we are blessed because it means that our victory is just around the corner.

In fact, many pastors will tell you that although God often waits until the last moment, He's never too late. God often allows everything to collapse and rescues us just in time. Sometimes our problems have nothing to do with us. God "hardened Pharaoh's heart" so that His plan could be instituted as an example for mankind. Jesus told His disciples that a certain person was blind not because of their sin or ancestral sin but for the purpose of manifesting His glory to give future generations hope and trust in Him.

Don't let doubt, frustration and fear defeat you. When things look the bleakest, remember the bigger the problem, the bigger the miracle. Try to find the lesson in every obstacle, the silver lining in every cloud. You will succeed. Didn't God promise that you are "more than a conqueror in Christ Jesus?" After all, the "battle belongs to the Lord," so quit your whining, relax and trust God. Tell yourself over and over that its now God's problem and He meant for you to be the head and not the tail. Don't act like a loser, you are a winner. As a child of the King of Kings you are to stand tall knowing that God loves you.

Above all else, do not give power to the enemy by fretting and speaking words of defeat and fear to yourself. Speak life and not death, victory and not defeat. Look forward and not backward.

So many times we are paralyzed by our past. We cannot believe that God has forgiven us because we haven't forgiven ourselves. We relive the past and our remorse threatens to drown us. *If only* is our password and we cannot move beyond the *if onlys* in our life. In fact, let me take this guilt paralysis one step further. Many times, our inability to accept the totality of God's forgiveness leads us to punish ourselves. Indeed, our bodies and minds work in such perfect synchronization that we can make ourselves sick. We don't need the devil or cigarettes to give us cancer; we are perfectly able to give it to ourselves through the power of our mind.

Let's get one thing straight. Although we are God's children, we don't deserve a miracle. Just as our children are not entitled to get whatever they want, we have no entitlement clause on our birth certificate. On the contrary, we have "all have sinned and fallen short of the glory of God" (Romans 3:23,NIV). Whether or not we get a miracle is God's call. Through the grace of God and the mighty work on the cross, God grants miracles. He forgives us our sins because of grace and the work on the cross. There are no good deeds we can do, no penance to promise, nor money to give that will produce a miracle or bring us forgiveness. God grants miracles because He loves us and because we call upon Him in faith and believe in His power to create a miracle.

Since 'goodness' doesn't bring a miracle you can quit worrying about being good enough or deserving enough. You aren't, but He can and will do it for you anyway because of His goodness. "It does not, therefore, depend on man's desire or effort, but on God's mercy" (Romans 9:16,NIV). We don't need to beat ourselves up anymore. To do so would be to deny the work on the cross and the awesome nature of God's mercy and grace.

God is the Alpha and Omega. His nature is circular, it has no beginning and it has no end. God just is. Since there is no one like God, we can rest confidant in knowing that there is no beginning or end to His mercy and grace. We can stop waiting for the sword of Damocles to fall. He is not punishing you; He is not going to punish you. He has already forgotten the sin you've confessed and repented. That is how much He loves you.

Enter into prayer confidant that you are "the righteousness of God". The Bible affirms that. As a believer in Christ Jesus, you are now clothed in His righteousness. Thank goodness we don't have to depend on our righteousness.

Now that you know your position in the heavens, stand strong against setbacks, praise God, thank Him for your miracle and expect those setbacks to vanish. The enemy cannot stand it when you praise God in every circumstance. He will flee. Anything that is of the light, like a positive mental attitude toward your problem, is something darkness and negativity can't stand. Throw out that defeatist attitude and speak words of victory. Remember that the fight is fixed. You are a winner because God is on your side. What do you have to worry about with God going before you?

God made you a winner. Claim that in the name of

Jesus. You "can do anything in Christ Jesus who strengthens" you. There is no mountain you can't climb, no ocean you can't swim across, no obstacle too great if you just believe.

Abraham, the father of both the Arabs and the Jews, is also considered the spiritual father of the Christians. God told Abraham he would become the father of many nations when Abraham was about a hundred years old and his wife, Sarah, about eighty. Despite their old age, Abraham "...did not waver through unbelief regarding the promise of God, but was strengthened in his faith and gave glory to God, being fully persuaded that God had power to do what He had promised" (Romans 4:18-21,NIV). Abraham believed despite physical circumstances that God could do the impossible.

Even so, God did not immediately answer his prayers or fulfill the promises He gave to him. Indeed, throughout the Bible are examples of how God made His people wait for the promises He gave to them. In speaking of Abraham and others in the Old Testament, the Bible said, "All these people were still living by faith when they died. They did not receive the things promised; they only saw them and welcomed them from a distance" (Hebrews 11:13,NIV).

God used these men and women of God to witness to us about the nature of faith so that we would be able to stand strong when trouble came. "Now faith is being sure of what we hope for and certain of what we do not see" (Hebrews 11:1,NIV). God wanted us to see that all the promises He made to His people were fulfilled in His time so that we could stand and be "certain of what we do not see." It is imperative that embodied within our confession of faith is this belief that the Lord has already ordered our miracle.

At times it is so hard to believe that the God who parted the Red Sea, rose from the dead and raised the dead would do a miracle for us in this day and age. We hear of miracles, but our disbelief holds us back. We try to find logical reasons for that which we cannot logically explain.

The first time I attended a healing service, I was filled with doubt. Even when the woman who God used as a healer called out my ailment in a group of just six people, I had a difficult time believing. When I pray and receive words from God, I question whether it truly is God talking or my 'flesh' talking. I constantly turn thoughts over and over in my head, dissecting them to ascertain whether or not I've made the entire thing up.

Recently I had an experience in hearing the voice of God. As I prayed for a friend, I thought God said to me, "I have a message for her son." Knowing this woman had more than one son I wondered which one God meant. A name popped into my head and I said, "I don't know if she has a son by that name." God then gave me a very disturbing picture that ended with a word of comfort.

All through the rest of my hike I kept wrangling with my thoughts. Finally, I said, "Okay God, if she's home when I get down from this hike, I'll believe this is a word from you. If she's not home, I'll just assume it was my mind talking." My friend wasn't home. I felt relieved. I didn't have to make a fool of myself after all.

Two weeks later, I ran into my friend and had an overwhelming urge to ask her if she had a son by the name God had given me. She did. I was so shocked that I told her what God had told me. God had told me that her son was desperate and at the end of the line. I could clearly see her son, gaunt, strung-out and full of despair. God wanted him to know that if he would turn to Him, He would save him once and for all. This time, if her son would seek God, he was sure to find the Lord. There was more to this message. I told her I would go home and write down everything the Lord had said to me and give her the letter to send to her son. Tears sprang to my friend's eyes, as she confirmed that it was a timely and accurate word. Her son had called her recently in desperate straits. She told me she would very much appreciate it if I would send her the letter for her son.

A very good friend and mentor of mine in Honolulu, Phyllis Ramia, has an awesome gift of prophecy. She told me that when she first became aware of this gift she would prophesy to the trees, to the ocean, to the sky and to the birds. She prophesied out loud because she felt the need to say it and not just think it. Yet, she was timid and uncertain of that which God was giving her and so she had to 'practice' by speaking to inanimate objects before she dared to tell people the words God was giving her. Now she operates with confidence, having seen thousands of prophetic words come true. Phyllis has gotten better at recognizing the voice of God prophesying through her.

We grow in the gifts of the Spirit if we practice. To practice means being positive and speaking out what we feel we have received. Our negative, disbelieving nature holds back our blessings, our gifts of the spirit and our miracle. Negative words empower the enemy. Since God lives in the praises of His people, it stands to reason that the enemy must flee when he hears God's people glorifying the King. It also makes sense that the enemy must live in the land of negativity.

Some Christian pastors believe that when you speak negativity, you are actually speaking curses over yourself and others. You are in effect, negating your miracle by the power of your words. The book of Proverbs says that you are "ensnared by the words of your mouth". Positive thoughts and words are blessings. Jesus himself tells us, "For out of the outflow of the heart the mouth speaks...For by your words you will be acquitted, and by your words you will be condemned" (Matthew 12:34-37,NIV). What comes out of your mouth, curses or blessings? Try to think about this before you speak over a matter.

My next door neighbor Jacque Wynne and I were giving a garden party with another friend and I looked up in the sky and said, "I hope it doesn't rain."

Jacque immediately said, "Don't say that. That's a negative thought. State the positive only. What a beautiful day it is. How lucky we are to have such a beautiful day for a party."

"It is written: 'I believed; therefore I have spoken.' With that same spirit of faith we also believe and therefore speak...Therefore we do not lose heart" (I Corinthians 4:13,NIV).

I have learned to speak positively and not negatively in all things. Do you constantly bemoan your fate or do you say, "A new day is coming." Do you speak curses or blessings to your children and your spouse? Do you constantly point out the negative or do you affirm that which is positive in their lives? People tend to knock themselves out for the one they love, if their loved one constantly reminds them how terrific they are. We want to be as good as how our loved one sees us. That is the power of the spoken word.

Keeping silent has a negative effect. The apostle James said. "You do not have because you do not ask God" (James 4:2,NIV). Verbalize as well as visualize what you want. Just going to the Lord in prayer is an act of faith. Over and over again in the Bible, Jesus told those who sought Him that their faith had healed them. When three blind men came to Him, Jesus asked them "Do you believe that I am able to do this?" When they answered affirmatively, He said, "According to your faith will it be done to you" (Matthew 9:28,29, NIV). We approach the Lord in faith, believing that He can do what we ask. By faith, believe that just by asking, we have received our miracle.

Pastor Dennis Leonard from Heritage Christian Center in Denver, admitted that many times he did not have the faith to believe God for a miracle in his life. However, he had the sense to say out of his mouth that which he desired, while thanking God for the answer to his prayer in advance. Even if you walk out the church doors sicker than when you went in, consider it a temporary setback and praise God for your healing despite how things look.

The book of Romans (NIV) tells us to "call things that are not as though they were". If there is something inside of you that doubts that God will work on your behalf to give you a miracle, thank Him anyway for the miracle as if it were a done deed. By speaking faith out of your mouth in prayer and supplication, faith will be added unto you.

Faith is the chapter in your life that defines you. It is the prologue to your book of life that colors your entire existence. Without faith, your book is superficial and without substance. It is not a literary work of which you may be proud.

Prayer is the seed we plant into the soil of faith. Praise and worship water the seed. The sun that breathes life into the plant is the light of Christ Jesus. Finally, the flowers that bloom as the result of all these component parts working together are the manifestation of those things that we desire—our miracle. Each part is essential to the miracle. You cannot have one without the other.

CHAPTER FIVE

DO I HAVE TO FORGIVE EVERYONE?

❖

"And when you stand praying, if you hold anything against anyone, forgive him so that your Father in heaven may forgive you your sins" (Mark 11:25,NIV).

Forgiveness. What does that have to do with a miracle?

God doesn't ask, He commands us to forgive others as a prerequisite to His forgiveness. Jesus said, "For if you forgive men when they sin against you, your heavenly Father will also forgive you. But if you do not forgive men their sins, your Father will not forgive your sins" (Matthew 6:14,15,NIV).

Years ago, I saw a couple on the 700 Club speak about losing their entire family in one hour. Their three young daughters came home from school one day and were brutally murdered by the neighbor's teenage son who went on a murderous rampage with a knife. It was a horrible story, but the couple's testimony left me feeling perplexed.

The couple testified that after a time of great bitterness and hatred for the boy who had killed their daughters, God began to change them. He began to put forgiveness in their heart for the boy and they even visited him in jail. They told the interviewer that they had forgiven him. I couldn't believe it. I thought the couple was nuts, deluded or just saying it for the benefit of TV. The only other explanation was that they were far better people than I could ever be.

The answer was "None of the above". The couple said that on their own, they couldn't do it. But with God's help, they learned to forgive this young man. The NIV Bible says, "I can do all things in Christ Jesus who strengthens me." We don't have to rely on our own ability or goodness, God provides His spirit through which we are able to do that which is impossible for us to do on our own.

God created man in His own image. Since that time, He has been trying to get us to get it. He wants us to be more like Him. He wants us to have His nature because if we did, we would be at peace. We battle so much because our 'sin nature' battles constantly with our 'god nature' and the internal strife interferes with God's wonderful plan for our lives.

To be more like Him we must learn the nature of forgiveness. God stands waiting for us to ask Him for forgiveness. He wants us to repent of our sins in order that He may show His great mercy and kindness by forgiving us of our sins. He sent "His only begotten son" (John 3:16,NIV), Jesus to earth as a man. He died on the cross as a living sacrifice for our sins. As I mentioned before, prior to Jesus' death, the Israelites were required to sacrifice a perfect, unblemished lamb to God as an offering for their sins. Through Jesus' sacrifice, we freely receive eternal life and salvation for our sins. Jesus was the final sacrifice. All of our sins are covered under this blood sacrifice. All we have to do is make a conscious effort to repent and ask for God's forgiveness in Jesus' name.

What about our own willingness to forgive others? If God is so gracious as to forgive us, can we do any less? Okay, so the person who hurt you doesn't deserve to be forgiven. I once read in a book that we should forgive "not because the person who hurt us deserves to be forgiven but because we don't deserve to feel that way anymore".

I can testify to that statement.

God gave me a very forgiving nature. I have been able to forgive everyone who has hurt me, no problem. I forgave the thief who stole a fortune in jewelry from me and even the man who date-raped me while I was in my 20's. However, I found it impossible to forgive the person who horribly abused my sons when they were very young children. I could not forgive him on my own. Especially since he seemingly escaped punishment for what he had done. For years I prayed for this individual like this: "God I forgive him. Except that you know that I don't really forgive him I'm only saying that because you told me that I had to forgive. Forgive me for my unforgiveness and help me to say 'I forgive him' and really mean it." Naturally I could not pray for salvation for this individual. Forget it, I was no saint. But God worked on me for years. Finally I was able to say, "Make him a new creation in Christ. And bless him too." Even as I said it, I immediately confessed to God that I wasn't really thinking that. I was more like Jonah who refused to go to Ninevah and warn the people that unless they turned from their ways, God would destroy them. Jonah was afraid that if the people did repent and ask God for forgiveness, God, being merciful and compassionate by nature, would not give them what Jonah considered their well-deserved punishment. In much the same way, I was afraid that God would save this person and that he would walk from his just punishment. I didn't want that to happen. I wanted him to suffer the way my sons had suffered. I wanted him to be punished. It wasn't fair that I had to pray that prayer. I had to admit that I felt it would be even more unfair if it was granted, and the man forgiven.

Years later, I ran into this individual and God instantly gave me a heart of forgiveness for him. I even prayed with him. I found that truly forgiving this person was a greater blessing to me than it was to him. I was delivered from years of bitterness, hatred and anger. All those emotions left me and I felt free for the first time in years. I could look at this individual without loathing filling my heart. Praise God, I was free! I even told someone, "If I had known how good I would feel, I would have done this sooner."

Forgive for yourself and the peace it will bring you. Complete forgiveness is impossible without God. Although it will not come easy, it will come in God's time. Say it out loud, "I forgive." Write the words on your heart and your deliverance will come. That deliverance is a miracle in and of itself.

God showed me during one of my hikes the nature of forgiveness. God's spirit of forgiveness flows through us like the river of life, watering the parched soil of our existence and bringing forth beautiful flowers. The flowers represent the beauty that springs from the arid soil through the nurturing spirit of forgiveness. The flowers are the fruits we receive when we forgive, along with gentleness, peace, compassion and mercy. They are also gifts of the spirit we receive through obedience to God. The miracle of our forgiving others brings forth incredible beauty and peace in our lives and sets the stage for our miracle.

Forgiveness paves the way for the miracle. Not only is it imperative that we forgive, it is imperative that we believe that we can receive complete and unequivocal forgiveness from the Lord. You must believe that you can receive forgiveness in order to give it back. God is not man. He is all power, all love and forgiveness. Say affirmatively, "I can do all things in Christ Jesus who strengthens me". You can learn to forgive. You can believe that God has forgiven you all things.

Sometimes we do not believe that God has forgiven us, therefore, we cannot forgive ourselves. Because of it, we do not accept the forgiveness that He freely gives. Don't beat yourself up. God forgave the Apostle Paul who was once in the business of killing Christians. There is nothing we have done that someone else has not already done that has not been completely and irrevocably forgiven by our great and glorious God. Remember that you are worthy of God's grace and goodness. You are worthy to receive his miracles because he made you worthy. "Not by works so that no one can boast", but by "grace you have been saved", the apostle Paul once said (Ephesians 2:8,9,NIV).

We have been forgiven of our sins, not because of us, but because of Jesus. "You are more than a conqueror through Him (Christ Jesus) that loves us" (Romans 8:37,NIV).

God loves you. He will "never leave you or forsake you" (Deuteronomy 31:6,NIV). No matter what you've done or will do, if you come to Him with a heart of repentance, "He will cleanse you from all unrighteousness" (Leviticus 16:30,NIV). You have been forgiven; all your sins are covered under Jesus' blood.

CHAPTER SIX

THE KINGDOM WITHIN
❖

Pray about what you want to be. You are what you pray. Your ally is your sub-conscious, the 'kingdom within'. That kingdom is truly within you. You just need to tap into it. God gave you an incredibly awesome gift, your mind. Psychologists say that the normal person uses only 10% of their brain. Imagine if we had the ability to tap into the other 90%.

Look at yourself without rationalization and take off those rose-colored glasses you wish you could hide behind. Make your prayer a practice in honesty by identifying those driving forces in your personality that prevent you from being all that you can be. That selfsame creative energy, misdirected, can be destructive. Take that energy and sublimate it into positive energy. Confess the thing you hate to admit. For example, "I hate my mother for abusing me as a child. I cannot forgive her for it." If need be, write it on a piece of paper and burn it, saying, "I give this sin to the Lord Jesus Christ who forgives me of it completely. I am now a new creation in Christ. I have been forgiven. This negative is no longer part of my life. I choose to enter God's kingdom by the blood of Jesus through which I have been saved. It's over; I do not ever have to think about this again. I have been irrevocably forgiven for hating my mother." My list of sins was three pages long, so don't feel bad. You must learn to look within and be absolutely truthful about yourself. Know who and what you are. God desires honesty above all things. He knows you're not perfect, but He loves you anyway.

The Bible is full of flawed men and women that God loved. Murderers, thieves, prostitutes and wastrels fill the pages of the Bible. What did Jesus say when he was criticized for hanging out with disreputable people? Jesus pointed out, "I did not come for the righteous. The righteous think they are righteous enough" (Matthew 9:13,NIV). He also said, "he who has been forgiven much, loves much" (Luke 7:47,NIV). Nowhere in the Bible does God say that He expects you to be perfect. In fact, He said that we "have all sinned and fall short of the glory of God" (Romans 3:23,NIV). Relax. There is nothing that we haven't done that God hasn't seen before. Despite everything that we've done, He's still willing to give us our miracle.

Now that you know that, you don't have to sugarcoat your motives and your actions. Be honest with God, He knows the truth anyway. He's God, He can read your mind and your heart so you might as well come clean with Him.

Through constant prayer, the Lord enables us to tap into that part of our brain that lies dormant. The power that lies therein represents the 'gifts of the Spirit' that Christians often talk about. When you accept Jesus, the power and indwelling of the Holy Spirit is there for the asking. You can ask God to allow you to receive the 'baptism of the Holy Spirit'. This baptism is a personal anointing from the Lord and gifts of the Spirit follow.

The gifts of the Spirit are listed in 1 Corinthians 12:8-10 (NIV). "To one there is given through the Spirit the message of wisdom...." This gift is the application of God's knowledge to everyday life. In a crisis situation we sometimes frantically leaf through the Bible looking for a message from God. Or, we spend hours on the phone or on the therapist's couch trying to find the answer to our problems. During times like this, God will often bring someone who may have a word for us from God that brings encouragement and clarity into our lives. How do we know God is using this person to bring us a word? We know it's from the Lord if it does not conflict with the Bible and it brings peace to our spirit.

Secondly, "...to another the message of knowledge by means of the same Spirit...." Again, the spirit of confusion causes a state of paralysis during times of stress. Our problems often demand that we make a choice and we find ourselves frozen by indecision. If we ask God for wisdom and knowledge, He will answer. Sometimes the answer comes from a third party, gifted in the word of wisdom and knowledge, who has intimate knowledge of our problems—even without our saying a word to them. This 'knowing' comes from the Holy Spirit. The best example of these gifts can be found watching the 700 Club when Pat Robertson and his fellow evangelists pray and receive 'words of knowledge' about people in the audience who are afflicted in various ways. During prayer, God reveals to them the various afflictions of various people and the ultimate outcome that God has ordained.

Some of the other gifts listed in 1 Corinthians (NIV) are self-explanatory; the gifts of faith, healing, miraculous power and prophesy. What may not be so clear is "...the ability to distinguish between spirits". There are many spirits in the spirit world. Our ability, for instance, to discern when someone is lying is a gift from God. Have you ever met someone that you disliked for no reason at all? Some Christians would say that your spirit discerned something in their spirit that warned you to stay away. One could say, for instance, that jury experts have the gift of discernment.

The ability to "speak in different kinds of tongues" and "the interpretation of tongues" are gifts that non-charismatic Christians and the non-Christians do not understand. Sometimes called the 'tongue of angels' or 'prayer language', tongues are a gift charismatic Christians seek. Some charismatics go so far as to say that one is not born again unless one has this particular gift. I don't agree. The gift of speaking in tongues is often given when people are in such extreme circumstances that they cannot even pray: their grief is too great. The Spirit of the Lord takes over and what comes out of them is what the apostle Paul referred to when he said, "For if I pray in a tongue, my spirit prays...." (I Corinthians 14:14,NIV). The interpretation of tongues is given to yet another person who suddenly understands and is able to perfectly translate that which is unintelligible to the rest of us.

The Spirit of the Lord gives one or more gifts to each individual. "All these are the work of one and the same Spirit, and he gives them to each one, just as he determines" (I Corinthians 12:11,NIV). The power is there for the asking. The Apostle Paul exhorts, "Follow the way of love and eagerly desire spiritual gifts, especially the gift of prophecy" (I Corinthians 14:1,NIV).

When you understand that the Lord God has given you power through the intercession of Jesus Christ and the Holy Spirit; you will be able to make your body cooperate with the desires of the deep mind. To truly work and operate in the gifts, there must be total surrender to the Lord God almighty. Then and only then will God lend you some of His tremendous power in order to do His will on earth. His will is to do miracles in your life. Believe that.

With your mind's eye, see yourself as you desire to be. This is prayer by affirmation. Visualize what you want for yourself and believe God will grant it. A friend of mine told me of her friend who had been told by the doctors that he had less than a year to live. He had systemic cancer that moved quickly throughout his entire body. He began to pray and visualize what God was doing for him while he prayed. Pac-man was a popular video game at the time. He began to visualize Pac-man eating the cancer in his body. Within six months, to his doctors' amazement, the cancer was completely gone.

A beautiful example of visualization reads, "the God who gives life to the dead and calls things that are not as though they were" (Romans 4:17,NIV). Do not be discouraged by the reality of the situation, visualize and vocalize what your vision is. Faith, hope and love must be at the center of our attention so that the sub-conscious mind can act upon your requests

It is important that you read and study the Bible. Combine your research with prayer and thereby focus your mind positively, affirming what you desire. By faith, the subconscious becomes our ally. Listen to that quiet, inner voice of your subconscious and believe that it is the Spirit of God, the kingdom within, directing you down life's path. Learn to listen to that still, quiet voice; submit it to God and go with it.

Faith comes by hearing the voice of God. Listen for it. Read His word. Find a church that feeds you the gospel of Jesus Christ. Stop, look and listen. God will begin to speak to you as you seek Him.

While hiking, I asked God to give me a revelation on prayer. The Lord gave me an amazing illustration on faith. God chooses certain people, like Benny Hinn and Sara O'Meara, to be healers. All the healing evangelists I know have said that God heals through them. Without God, they are just ordinary people. Healers are, in a sense, channelers of God's power. The spirit of healing flows through them into other people.

The Lord showed me healers are faucets turned on by God. The water flowing through is God's spirit and the sprinkler system it feeds into is faith. God's power to heal flows from the healer to the seeker but faith within the seeker is what makes the spirit flow through their entire body and creates the healing.

This principle was made clear for me one morning when my housekeeper came to work sick. God has blessed me with Christian housekeepers whenever He knew I would need one. On that particular day, Sylvia told me that she almost didn't make it to work because she wasn't feeling well. I immediately felt compelled to tell her, "Let's pray." Interestingly enough, Sylvia later told me that as soon as she walked into the house, she felt God tell her, "Go to Carole's bedroom and have her pray for you." She didn't tell me because she wanted to see if God would prompt me.

When Sylvia and I pray together, it's very funny. She prays in Spanish and I pray in English. We also both pray in tongues and it can sound quite confusing. But we are in accordance in spirit, and that's what matters. We prayed together that morning and fifteen minutes later she reported, "I'm feeling better." By the time she left, she had a big smile on her face and she said, "I'm well."

God reminded me that Jesus told many people, "Your faith has healed you." I was the faucet; the spirit flowed through my pipes and entered Sylvia whose faith watered her entire body. I thanked God for using me to heal Sylvia who had the faith to believe in her healing.

A friend of mine once told me, "I wish God would talk to me the way He talks to you." Lest you think I feel I am special, I want you to know God does not select only a few people to listen to. He is a democratic God, offering His ear and hand to anyone who will call upon Him and seek Him with all their hearts.

God will talk to anyone who will listen. There are no magic words. God is a gentleman; He will not barge into your life without asking. Ask, seek and knock. The more you pray, the more you listen, you will begin to hear that still, quiet voice that wells from your heart. This voice will bring you an incomparable peace that will lift you up no matter how discouraged you are. God offers you a "peace of God, which transcends all understanding" (Philippians 4:7,NIV). Pastor Dennis Leonard of the Heritage Christian Center calls it that "crazy peace", a peace that defies your circumstances. The peace that comes from knowing that you are in the center of God's will and that He is in control, no matter how bad things look in the present. It is a peace that says, "I am in the middle of the worst storm in my life but I can rest knowing that Jesus is in the boat with me."

Jesus slept while a furious squall rocked the boat He and

His disciples were in. The disciples were so afraid they woke Him and said, "Teacher, don't you care if we drown?" Jesus got up and calmed the storm. Then He turned to His disciples and said "Why are you so afraid? Do you still have no faith?" (Mark 4:35-40,NIV)

Open your consciousness to the Lord and listen for instruction and wisdom. There is an old Indian saying, "Listen, or thy tongue will keep thee deaf." Listen for that voice. Jesus said, "My sheep know my voice." I have often felt that I was doing something wrong because I wasn't sure if I was talking to myself or if God was talking, or if the enemy was misleading me. I agonized over it and finally, the Lord gave me peace about it. When I pray, I put every word, every thought, every deed, every action and vision into obedience in Christ Jesus. I asked God to let only His thoughts enter my head. Then whatever I think or feel after that, I go with it and try not to doubt.

The voice of God is your thoughts, feelings, impulses and intuition. One way to know if God is talking is that He will never contradict the Bible. In addition, thoughts that are negative, self destructive and accusatory are from the devil. The devil will tell you, "God doesn't love you. He won't answer your prayers: you're too bad for Him to give you the time of day, let alone answer your prayers." Cast that negative thinking aside. Jesus said, "Get thee behind me, Satan." Tell the devil to get out of your thoughts. Invoke the name of Jesus and tell the devil you're not listening to negativity. Remember God made you, and He's not in the business of making rubbish. He sent Jesus to save sinners. He loves you; He will always love you, even when you make the wrong choices. He wants all of us to repent, accept the blood sacrifice on the cross and turn to Him for everything. You are a child of God and He will love you no matter what.

No negative thoughts should receive your direct attention for too long. If we persist in giving these demons or negative thoughts our attention, we block ourselves by denying that we have received our answer. God cannot work in an atmosphere of doubt and unbelief. When you give the demons of negative thoughts too much attention, you are giving them power over your life. In a sense, you are paying unconscious tribute to the power of negative thoughts.

Accept the power of prayer. Believe you have received. Do not limit God's effectiveness by denying that he can do the whole job. Believe that prayer is capable of producing what you desire. The idea is that which is invisible, the visible manifestation is prayer. This requires understanding, principle and effort. Everything in life stands on the principles of cause and effect. Prayer is the cause; the effect is the answer to these prayers. Hold this principle close to your heart and believe that prayer will bring you answers.

Act as if you have received-no matter what happens. Thank God in advance for the answer to your prayer. "Thank you Lord for healing me." Jesus instructs, "When you pray, believe that you have received and it will be done by my Father in heaven." The answer is on its way; it's a done deal. Believe it and affirm it with your mouth by thanking God for your miracle before it arrives. Sometimes we need to write things down and place it before us to remind ourselves that we believe God for certain miracles.

Remember that the enemy does not want you to receive answers to prayers. He will throw up stumbling blocks and setbacks. They are just temporary. God allows it to strengthen our faith. Even if the gates of hell come against you and the very opposite of what you are praying for happens, affirm your prayer and accept it within. Believe and your prayer will manifest itself visibly, that is one of the secrets to miracles.

CHAPTER SEVEN

POWER IN NUMBERS

❖

Many charismatic Christians stand on Jesus' promise: "Again, I say unto you that if two of you shall agree on earth as touching anything that they shall ask, it shall be done for them of my Father which is in heaven" (Matthew 18:19, King James Version only).

This is why many Christians hold hands and pray and why many of them will touch an object, like a piece of paper with the promises written on it, and pray over it. Jesus also said, "For where two or three come together in my name, there am I with them" (Matthew 18:20,NIV).

Now we come to the subject of prayer groups. There is great power in prayer groups. My first exposure to the power of prayer groups came about spontaneously. My mother had a dinner party at which my brother arrived in visible pain. I asked him what was wrong and he replied, "I have to go in for back surgery this week." For some reason, I felt compelled to gather my brother, my sisters and my mother into the master bedroom to do something we had never done before; lay hands on my brother and pray as a family for his healing. Now, my brother had been miraculously delivered from a 20-year cocaine addiction by the Lord, and consequently became born again. Knowing the power of God, he was willing for us to pray over him.

Honestly, we didn't know what to do. We just made a

circle around him, touched him with our hands and prayed. Looking at him expectantly after the prayer I said, "Well, did you feel anything?"

My brother looked at me curiously and said, "I think I feel better."

"Think?" I replied with disappointment. "Don't you know?"

"I think I'm better," was all he had to say.

The next day, my brother called me and said, "You won't believe this."

I was excited. "Now do you know that you feel better?"

My brother laughed. "Not only do I know that I feel better, I just came from the doctor who gave me more X-rays and he said I don't need the surgery after all."

"Really?" I exclaimed.

"He asked me what I had done, because the two sets of X-rays didn't even look like the same back. So I told him that my sisters and my mother prayed over me and I woke up this morning able to walk straight."

The doctor said that whatever my brother had done had obviously worked. Praise God! We didn't even know what we were doing. That's okay, God looks at the heart and not the format.

If you desire a special anointing, join an intercessory prayer group of spirit-filled Christians and watch the miracles flow into your life. The Bible says, "How could one man chase a thousand, or two put ten thousand to flight" (Deuteronomy 32:30, NIV). When you come into agreement in prayer, there is great power. Didn't God promise, "where two or more are gathered in my name," He would be there?

God loves it when we gather in His name and spend

time worshipping and praising Him. In doing this, we don't have to worry about getting everything just right. God showed me a marvelous example of that when I went to see Benny Hinn at a healing service in Albuquerque.

A woman came up to the stage and claimed a miraculous healing. The scene that ensued seemed so staged and phony that my mother and I became increasingly uncomfortable. We began to doubt the entire service because of this one woman. The euphoria we had felt during the last two services began to evaporate. At the time, we had no idea each of us was feeling the same thing. We discussed our discomfort with each other later on that night before going to bed, troubled by the same question. Was the whole crusade a fake?

That night, I felt the Lord speak to me. "Did you see thousands of people seeking me, praising me, thanking me and adoring me?" I told the Lord I did. "Did you feel the presence of the Holy Spirit in that place." The Lord continued to ask forcefully. Again, I agreed. "Then what did it matter if one woman decided to use the service as her stage? Do not let one woman ruin the entire crusade for you."

I stopped and thought, "That's right. What does it matter?" I felt God in the Tingley Coliseum and witnessed very real healings. I saw very young children of four or five years old throw away their leg braces and crutches and walk for the first time. I saw these precious boys and girls overcome with emotion and sobbing so hard they couldn't even talk. That was real. I felt it in my spirit.

God continued forcefully, "What mattered were the thousands of people seeking me, praying to me, loving me, praising me and thanking me. That was real. That was what mattered."

I knew then that I was hung-up on the details. Now may I say that the Lord was not saying that Benny Hinn was a fake. On the contrary, Benny Hinn is anointed by God and what I witnessed there in New Mexico was truly miraculous. The Lord was merely pointing out an important principle. The worshipful attitude of thousands of people coming in agreement was what was important.

There will always be a few fakers and spoilers among the thousands. At that same service, a young woman with four small children under the age of 6 sat behind me and spent most of the service cursing her children, which, of course, distracted everyone around her. I began to pray against the distraction and bless her and her children. Within fifteen minutes of my prayer, the woman became silent. Later, I observed her staring at me with something close to hostility but she remained silent for the rest of the service. I praised God for silencing her and ridding all of us of the distraction. My mother and friend later told me that they had started praying for her just before she stopped her cursing.

Don't let the spoilers in the kingdom stop your praises and prayers. There is enormous strength in numbers. The singing and praises of the multitude set up the healers for victory prior to the actual healings. Every single person at Benny Hinn's crusade was a vital part of the miraculous healings that took place. All of us played an anointed part during those three days in Albuquerque.

Back to intercessory prayer groups. There are prayer lines all over America. Benny Hinn, the 700 Club, and your local church all have one. If you don't belong to one and are in crisis, reach out to them. They are available to pray for you 24 hours a day. They are your lifelines in times of need.

However, if it is a miracle you need in your life then you need to join a prayer group. Prayer groups only require people who seek God with "all their hearts, all their minds and all their soul" because they cannot do it themselves anymore. If you don't know any, start one with another spirit-filled Christian. All you need is two of you coming in agreement in prayer. Commit to praying for each other at least once a week and then DO IT. There is nothing like the "fervent prayers of a righteous man," according to the Word, to move God's heart. Since we have been made righteous in Christ Jesus and don't have to depend on our own righteousness, we can count ourselves as righteous. After all, God calls us the "righteousness of God" in the Bible.

I'm hooked on prayer groups. I know that God loves it when His people gather together in His name and with praise and thanksgiving seek Him.

In the 1950's, a psychology professor at the University of Redlands found his life spinning out of control as he headed for a nervous breakdown. On top of that, he developed painful ulcers. A 'Sunday-only' Christian, he began to pray to get well as a last resort. He sought God earnestly for the first time because of the inability of science to cure his ulcer and because he felt headed for a nervous breakdown. Miraculously, he was healed. As a consequence of the curious nature of his healing, he decided to study prayer from a scientific standpoint.

First, he obtained permission from the University of Redlands to run his experiment. His 'guinea pigs' were volunteers obtained from advertisements within the campus and recommendations from doctors and therapists around the town. Every single volunteer had one thing in common.

They were desperate and at the end of their rope. They had tried everything and failed. Their doctors had ruled their cases hopeless and in many cases, terminal.

The professor set up three groups. The first group committed to meetings, once a week, for an entire year. During the course of the year, they committed to praying for themselves and each other as a group. The second group were people who said they would pray solo. The third group included people who committed to seeing a psychotherapist once a week for a year instead of praying. The results were astonishing.

Almost every single person in the prayer group was healed. One young wife and mother came for her husband, a professor, who had refused to join and who was diagnosed with terminal cancer while still in his early 30's. Even this man was healed.

No one was healed in the second group who prayed for themselves. I found this absolutely amazing at first. I know many people who have prayed for themselves and/or others, solo and received miracles.

Do not think that if you pray solo nothing will happen. There were reasons that the people who prayed solo in that study did not get healed, but it does not invalidate the ability of God to work through a single person's prayers. Often, when people begin to pray for themselves, they pray 'amiss'. They pray with wrong motives, with double-mindedness or they lack faith. When you pray for yourself, it is important that you ask other people to pray for you and to cover you with that which you lack in yourself.

In both the psychotherapy and the prayer groups, the same number of people were healed. The difference was that once the people who saw psychotherapists stopped seeing their doctors, they relapsed or became sick with something else. Only the first group experienced complete and unequivocal healings.

You can read about these fascinating and miraculous experiments in the book Prayer Can Change Your Life by William R. Parker and Elaine St. Johns. Unfortunately, you may have to borrow it at the library. Being a Psychology Major, it is one of my favorite books on prayer as it incorporates scientifically gathered data using very specific controls that combine science, psychology and spirituality.

Interestingly, most of the people in the first group did not start as even nominal Christians. They were desperate people who had no hope and were willing to try anything. I find that God often waits until you're on the steps of the courthouse before He intervenes. Perhaps He's trying to teach us lessons of hope, perseverance and faith. What do you think? Are you desperate enough for a miracle? Then let us take further steps to the miracle-now.

CHAPTER EIGHT

GIVE IT TO GOD
❖

Give God your hate, your problems, your illnesses, your insecurities, everything. He loves you yesterday, today, tomorrow, and forever. He wants to carry your burdens. Jesus said, "Come to me, all you who are weary and burdened, and I will give you rest" (Matthew 11:28,NIV). No matter what you are carrying, believe that He loves you and will carry you through your problems. This is the peace many Christians have when going through the most horrendous circumstances. We know God is with us, He loves us, He forgives us, and He is in control. We know from the psalmists in Ecclesiastes that there is a "season for everything under the heavens". We know that this too will pass, and it is just a millisecond in eternity, which, in the scheme of life, is nothing. "Meaningless", say the psalmists. "There is a time for everything", and a purpose to everything. Trust God and go on with your life knowing that He's in charge.

Jesus told His disciples in chapter 12 of the book of Luke (NIV): "Therefore I tell you, do not worry about your life, what you will eat; or about your body, what you will wear. Life is more than food and the body more than clothes. Consider the ravens: they do not sow or reap, they have no storeroom or barn; yet God feeds them. And how much more valuable you are than birds!"

In that same chapter, Jesus also pointed out another

important principle, "But seek His kingdom, and these things will be given to you as well." God will supply you everything, "according to His riches and glory" if you seek Him first. Seeking His kingdom means doing His will in your life, glorifying and serving Him. This is what James meant when he said, "Faith without works is dead."

Receive the things you have affirmed for yourself and turn everything over to God. Receive His guidance, inspiration and renewal and let guilt go. Don't be afraid to tell God everything, he already knows it anyhow and understands. He doesn't expect us to be perfect. He knows how imperfect we are.

The world looks at born again Christians and see a repressive life full of rules and regulations. The truth is there is great freedom in following Jesus. We have discovered a very elementary truth: if we follow the Lord our life does get easier and we thereby gain more choices in our lives. The reason we stop doing the things we used to do, like going to bars or sleeping around with different partners is because it doesn't feel good to do it anymore. There is such peace in doing it God's way; we do not feel any loss.

The love of God fills our life in such a way that we do not miss that which we gave up. We choose God's way and gain so much by it.

The greatest freedom we obtain through our new life in Jesus is freedom from our past. Knowing that we have been forgiven for all of our sins and are now truly a 'new creation in Christ', frees us from the burden of our sins and sin nature. To not believe that we are totally forgiven is to deny the power of the cross. It is to deny that the sacrifice of our Lord was insufficient to meet the penalty of our sins.

Moreover, it is to deny the power behind the miracle.

We are often hamstrung by our own doubts and insecurities as well as by our past. We are the sum total of all of our past experiences. Sometimes we have difficulty forgiving others and ourselves for hurtful experiences we cannot put aside. We allow the past to shape our future by messing up our present. The freedom the cross represents is deliverance once and for all. We no longer have to look back, the slate has been wiped clean and we have been delivered from the memories that held us hostage. The bitterness we felt in the past is released once and for all and our bad memories cannot color our lives anymore. Because the King of Kings loves us, we are free.

Recognize that not only does God know us, He is within us, ever present, ever willing and ever able to heal us, cast out demons and create a miracle. Honestly evaluate what rules our consciousness and seek to keep our eye on Jesus rather than our symptoms and problems. Don't even pray about your symptoms, it is reaffirming the negative in your life. "I am healed," should be your prayer of affirmation.

One final note on 'giving it to God'. Are you able to give your problem to God without giving Him the answer to the question? Or do you pray like this, "Dear God, this is my problem and this is the way I want you to answer it." I recently heard a song on the radio that went something like this, "Sometimes the greatest gift God gives you are unanswered prayers." Interesting concept. Unlike the lyricist, I believe God answers every prayer. However, at times the answer is 'no'. Can you accept no for an answer or must you have it your way?

Giving it to God means leaving the entire matter in His hands. After all, He's God. Isn't it possible that He knows what's best for you in spite of yourself? I can honestly say that in my past there have been people and things that I absolutely had to have. In retrospect, not getting it changed my life. My life was better for it. Give it to God and walk away.

CHAPTER NINE

LOVE IS NOT A CHOICE

❖

In order to receive our miracle, we must enter the circle of love. Jesus said, "A new command I give you. Love one another. As I have loved you, so you must love one another" (John 13:34,NIV). The Greeks have three different words for love. The most perfect, God-like love is called agape. We strive for that. Lacking the ability to manifest love as perfectly as God, we ask Him to let His love permeate us. Surrender will follow when we enter God's circle of perfect love. We should remove everything in our lives that we hate and allow God to replace it with the Holy Spirit.

We love Him because He loved us first. Accept love just as you are, because God loves you with all your shortcomings. Its sometimes difficult to believe that God loves us, and, therefore, we reject His love. At the same time, we often unwittingly reject other people's love because we find ourselves unlovable or unworthy of love. If we don't love ourselves, how can anyone else love us? Keep in mind that we are worthy because of God's love. We don't have to be perfect; no one is or ever was except Jesus. This sounds so simple, yet sometimes we don't even realize that we don't love ourselves. Accept this if you can, God loves you because He made you with all your flaws. Pastor Leonard loves to say, "God made you and He doesn't make rubbish."

If you can love yourself, you can love others. Tell yourself, "I love because the way to love is to start loving." Love reflects love. Love for God makes you want to be more perfect. When you were little, you did things to please your earthly father because you loved him. As we grow up in Christ, we begin to love Him more and more and that love makes us want to please Him.

The fruit of love is loyalty, self-sacrifice and forgiveness. Once you receive the miracle of forgiveness, your enemies lose the power to hurt you. God takes those burdens and you will rarely ever think about them again. It is a finished work in your life and you will be able to move on.

There is no limit to the power of love. We open ourselves through prayer to experience God's love. Through deep desire, prayer and insisting that we love God with all our hearts, mind and strength, we become that which we affirm. The power of love will teach us to be masters in the art of loving. We can use as a measure of love; loyalty, sacrifice and forgiveness. These are the ways that we can measure our present relationships. Let the ingredients of love filter through our every thought and deed, then act as if this were a fact.

With gratitude and thanksgiving, we can observe the love bestowed upon us by others and follow this all the way to Jesus until an answering love floods our being and we pray to become worthy channels through which this inspiration may pass to others. As we praise and thank Jesus, He answers us by filling us with His perfect love. We should then love because we are loved. We are loved because we love.

However, even the love of God is only manifested and

mediated through people. Ask God to become more loving and in faith, act as if it were already true.

Pollyanna was loved by so many because she loved openly, guilelessly and without expectation. If we effectively channel the unconditional love of God we will draw people to us like a magnet because love is a circle. The more we give, the more we get. Unlovable people are unable to manifest love. They do not know how to love.

God gave my brother-in-law Jerel Miller an example of loving someone who appeared to be unlovable, when he began work as a youth pastor at a poor, small church in San Diego. He met a surly boy of 17 who smelled because he was living in his car, having been kicked out of his home because he refused to comply with his parents' rules. He had one pair of pants that he sometimes took to a stream to wash and only came to the youth group for the free food they served during the meetings. At first Jerel was repulsed by this young man who openly admitted he didn't believe in God, he just wanted the food.

I commented, "Perhaps God is testing you by bringing you someone so hard to love." Both Jerel and my sister, Sandy agreed and reminded themselves that Jesus said, "He who is forgiven much, loves much." They began to pray for him and show love to him, despite their initial revulsion. They even bought him some deodorant. Within a couple of weeks of letting this boy hang out with Jerel, he suddenly moved back home and became one of the most enthusiastic members of the youth group. Love brings out the best in people; it can turn their lives around. My sister Sandy and her husband now truly love that boy they were first repulsed by.

One of the most quoted chapters in the Bible is I Corinthians 13 (NIV), often called the love chapter. Let me repeat it: "If I speak in the tongues of men and of angels, but have not love, I am only a resounding gong or a clanging cymbal. If I have the gift of prophecy and can fathom all mysteries and all knowledge and if I have a faith that can move mountains, but have not love, I am nothing. If I give all I possess to the poor and surrender my body to the flames, but have not love, I gain nothing.

"Love is patient, love is kind. It does not envy, it does not boast, it is not proud. It is not rude, it is not self-seeking, it is not easily angered, and it keeps no record of wrongs. Love does not delight in evil but rejoices with the truth. It always protects, always trusts, always hopes, and always perseveres.

"Love never fails. But where there are prophecies, they will cease; where there are tongues, they will be stilled' where there is knowledge, it will pass away. For we know in part and we prophesy in part, but when perfection comes, the imperfect disappears. When I was a child, I talked like a child, I reasoned like a child. When I became a man, I put childish ways behind me. Now we see but a poor reflection as a mirror, then we shall see face to face. Now I know in part; then I shall know fully, even as I am fully known.

"And now these three remain: faith, hope and love. But the greatest of these is love."

Pastor Earl Takaoka, of Harvest Chapel in Honolulu, shared one of the best illustrations of love I've ever heard. He told the story of a woman, who married 'the love of her life,' had three children and felt her life couldn't be happier. One day, her husband was given an assignment in Japan for a short period of time. They both decided that she should stay in Hawaii with the children rather than displace them.

Months passed and she received a letter that broke her heart. Her husband told her that he had fallen in love and wanted a divorce. When she told her children of their father's decision to stay in Japan, one of them asked, "Just because daddy doesn't love us anymore, does that mean we can't love him?"

Years passed and the man had three children with his new wife, when another shattering letter arrived in Hawaii. The man had terminal cancer and his finances were not what they should have been. Would his ex-wife possibly consider helping them financially? As she read the letter, the woman thought of what her child had said years ago, "Just because daddy doesn't love us, does that mean we can't love him anymore?" Looking at the photograph her ex-husband had enclosed, her eyes filled with tears as she saw her husband in each of his three children.

She wrote back that she would help them as best she could. However, she felt that she could best help them in Hawaii. With steely determination, she began the lengthy immigration process for his new family. After he died, she brought her ex-husband's new wife and three children to Hawaii to live with her. Love never dies. Sometimes it evolves into different forms, but real love remains the one constant in life that every human being yearns for.

God is calling you into His circle of love. Jesus said, "Thou shalt love the Lord your God with all your heart and with all your soul and with all your mind. This is the first and greatest commandment. And the second is like it: 'Love your neighbor as yourself.' All the Law and the Prophets hang on these two commandments" (Matthew 22:37-40,NIV).

St. Augustine said, "Love and do what you like." Love covers all things. If you love, the effect is "goodness and light."

There is no limit to the power of love for we are nothing without love. In studies done in orphanages in developing countries, it was found that babies who were not held and cuddled but merely had their physical needs taken care of suffered mentally, physically and emotionally. We perish for lack of love. Love is the single most redeeming factor on earth. It is the salvation of mankind in a world spinning out of control fast. When Jesus' exhorted His followers to "turn the other cheek," He was really talking about showing love to "those that hurt us." Love was Jesus' message. It is the implementation of such selfless agape love (God's love in Greek) we find impossible. However, as the old saying goes, "love has it's own rewards."

Pastor J.P. Woods from Aspen Christian World Outreach gave a splendid example of the power of love. While he was ministering at the Pitkin County jail, J.P. was told that a man who had spent eleven years in prison had 'freaked out' and destroyed the premises around him while beating two of his jailers. It had taken five sedatives to calm him down. At that time, he was in lock-down, strapped to a chair from head to toe. They had even put a mouth guard on him to prevent him from swallowing his tongue. JP asked to see the prisoner but was told it was much too dangerous. Finally, JP persuaded them that anyone who attended outlaw biker rallies had God's protection. The jailers reluctantly agreed and let him see the prisoner with the door ajar while they stood by.

Before seeing the prisoner, JP began to pray. I cannot

overemphasize how important it is to cover whatever you do in prayer. Sara O'Meara, a healer who began Child-Help, a charitable organization that aids abused children, prays diligently before her healing services. Every man and woman of God begins any venture with prayer.

JP saw the man sedated, but still hostile. JP became filled with the love and compassion of Jesus Christ as he began to minister to this man. Discovering that this man's entire family had turned their backs on him, JP told him that although his actions were wrong, God loved him in spite of it. Instead of judging this man, God filled JP with a corresponding love that flowed from JP to this man. During the hour they spent together, the man calmed down and by the end of the session, he was begging JP to come back to visit him again. Love begets love. Love is transforming. Love is the only thing that can change a person from a wild beast to a man.

Praise God for the love you feel and have been shown and you will bring love to you. Love attracts love in return. You will draw love to you by manifesting love to someone else even if you don't feel love at first. The benefits, to you too, will be enormous.

I am reminded of a young woman I know in Aspen who lives in a mansion. I ran into her and thanked her for donating so much money to Challenge Aspen, a charitable organization I had been involved with that helps the handicapped find new life in sports, the arts and music. This young woman who had everything money could buy smiled and told me that she had volunteered at the Challenge Aspen camp the day before and worked with some of the handicapped children. "I'm going back tomorrow," she informed me excitedly. "It felt so good to get my hands dirty and do something for someone else."

The benefit to you in reaching out with love to someone else is incalculable. You will feel good about yourself.

If you feel that no one loves you, remember that God loves you unconditionally. He made you and the Bible promises that "He will never leave you nor forsake you" (Deuteronomy 31:6,NIV). If you want to be loved, reach out and love someone without an ulterior motive. Visit the homeless, the sick, the elderly or anyone else that is basically ignored in this world and reach out in love to them. I assure you that you will find a wealth of love waiting to embrace you. You will find that love given out will be returned tenfold.

You don't have to feel lonely and unloved anymore. Get out of yourself and stop crying about how alone and unhappy you are. By doing so, you are reaffirming the negative in your life and giving power to it. Begin to thank God for His love and the power of love to transform. Thank Him for bringing love back into your life by giving you the ability to love selflessly. Thank Him for surrounding you with people to love. Then get out there and show your love to a hurting world.

Love, and it will be given back to you, I promise.

CHAPTER TEN

GOD CAN USE ANYONE

❖

You are vital to the king and to His kingdom. Never lose sight of your importance to Him. You are cleansed, a 'new creation in Christ', worthy because of Jesus' righteousness to take your place next to the throne of God. Whenever you feel depressed, remember that you are a child of God and praise Him in thanksgiving for this awesome gift.

Every time you ask God to forgive you of all your sins through the blood of Jesus, you are cleansed and made righteous. Through this forgiveness, you are able to enter the throne room of God and give Him your prayers and petitions. Every time we pray, we are entering the "Holy of Holies," the throne room of God. This is your legacy as God's child. To deny that God has totally and irrevocably erased all of your sins and remembers them no more is to deny the power of the cross and the incredible work that Jesus did for our sake. So do not doubt that God has forgiven us so completely that it is as if it had never happened. To doubt that is to doubt God Himself.

Chapter 3 of the book of Romans (NIV) explains this principle beautifully: "This righteousness from God comes through faith in Jesus Christ to all who believe. There is no difference, for all have sinned and fall short of the glory of God, and are justified freely by His grace through the redemption that came by Christ Jesus. God presented Him as a sacrifice of atonement, through faith in His blood...God will credit righteousness—for us who believe in Him who raised Jesus our Lord from the dead...Therefore, since we have been justified through faith, we have peace with God through our Lord Jesus Christ through whom we have gained access by faith into this grace in which we now stand."

Therefore, before we stand in His throne room, cast aside all your doubts. Be like-minded with your prayer partners and confess that God is all you need. He wants to bless you. He wants to help you. All you have to do is ask.

God loves using the simple people of the world to do miracles. After all, Christ used fishermen and farmers, not the ruling elite of Israel. When He went back to the Father, He promised that we would do "greater things than these, because I (Jesus) am going to the Father."

I've often heard, "God wouldn't use me." I myself have said that. Sara O'Meara points out that in saying that we deny the power of God. An all-powerful God can use anybody. In fact, God often "chooses the foolish things of the world" (I Corinthians 1:27,NIV) or the most unlikely people with a past to do His will so that the miracle might be even greater. Let me take the time to give you examples of how God uses the most unlikely people.

One of my friends is a beautiful woman who has been married and divorced three times. She is a woman who loves and trusts the Lord. Her testimony has taught me lessons in trusting God and not in one's circumstances.

Years ago, her husband lost his high paying job, and, soon after that, was arrested for drug trafficking. His story was on the front page of the local newspaper. They went from living in a big house and driving fancy cars to being literally down to their last penny. Instead of panicking, she trusted God to meet her family's needs on a daily basis and to deliver her husband from his legal problems. Trusting God in spite of their dire circumstances, God miraculously came through for them and her husband was found innocent.

Divorced for the third time, God continues to use her as a wonderful witness to His faithfulness no matter what the circumstances. She and her former husband, who is now a pastor, have given their testimony on the 700 Club.

Another friend of mine, Colleen Nomura, is a beautiful divorcee who has worked as a professional dancer and choreographer. Before she became a Christian, Colleen lived a wild life. Raised a Buddhist, she lived a 'glamorous', hedonistic life, going from man to man and frequenting the bars after working hours.

We attended college together during the 'hippie years'. All three of us wear mini-skirts and make-up. We diligently work at keeping up a youthful appearance. We love to dance and go out. When God called us to work in His kingdom, we had our doubts. Our first reaction was, "You're kidding. You couldn't possibly be calling me."

Colleen was the first to quit her career and went to work as a missionary for twelve years. Living with her boyfriend at the time, she moved out, stopped picking up guys at bars and got into the Bible to prepare herself for a life of ministry. Her life turned on a dime.

It wasn't so easy for my other friend and I. When God called us, we resisted. "Look God," I argued, "we're not the type. I mean, look at us. We don't look or act like your typical servants of the Lord. We're divorcees who like to party and have a good time. We're not exactly holy. People will really criticize us for trying to witness when we are so far from perfect." When I said that, I thought of the pastor's wife I knew when I was a child. In my opinion, she was what a pastor's wife should look and act like. In these times though, we might as well throw our preconceived notions of what pastors' wives should look and act like out the window. My sister Sandy, a former flight attendant, works out, wears make-up and is very glamorous. Out of deference to her husband Jerel and his profession, she dresses much more conservatively than she did in the past. One of the best rock and roll dancers you've ever seen, Sandy looks and acts young and hip.

Having been through a series of dysfunctional relationships with abusive men before meeting Jerel, she is able to relate in a powerful way to young women with similar problems. While still in high school, she attempted suicide by swallowing a full bottle of pills. She also suffered from bulimia. All of those negatives become positives when applied to her work with hurting teenage girls in her ministry. She is able with connect to them in arenas that are mystifying to the typical pastor's wife.

Another atypical pastor's wife is Aspen Pastor JP Wood's wife Donna, once a singer in a rock band. As befits the stereotype, she did cocaine, drank and even got involved in witchcraft. Sexually assaulted as a girl of twelve years, her witness is powerfully moving. God uses the terrible things in our lives to bring healing to others. The more awful the experience, the more awesome the witness.

So often, we feel that because of our past, we are not worthy to be used in God's kingdom. May I remind you that

God loves you, just as you are. In fact, He uses you mightily because of your past.

Sandy and Donna are only two examples of women who look nothing like a pastor's wife. In fact, both women said that if someone had told them prior to meeting their husbands that they would someday be pastors' wives, they would have either laughed or run in the other direction.

Let me add that both their husbands do not look like typical pastors. Jerel is a super athlete with movie star good looks. Then there's JP with his long, white ponytail who looks like the biker/hippie he was when he was 'in the world'. When Christians talk about being 'in the world', they are referring to their lives before they found God.

The interesting thing about God is that He uses whomever He wants. He also uses those people that don't think they can or should be used. When Moses was told by God via the burning bush to go back to Egypt and deliver His people, Moses made excuses. Moses told God He wasn't capable of such a great commission because he stuttered. But God wouldn't listen to excuses. He sent Moses to Pharaoh with his brother Aaron, to do the talking for him.

Jonah didn't want to go to Ninevah and was put in the belly of a whale. There have been times in my life when I felt like I was in the belly of a whale because I resisted the idea of God's using me for so long. He will put you in situations and places until you say, "Okay, God. I give up. Whatever." He does have a way of getting your attention.

I remember my thrice-divorced friend saying to me, "I just want to find a nice Christian man to marry. I'm not made for a great calling on my life."

I agreed. "Neither am I. I don't want it. I never asked for

it. It's too great a responsibility." So here I am writing this book that I didn't want to write because I didn't feel qualified enough to write it, having no divinity training. Besides, I didn't want to expose myself this way. I wanted to remain a private person.

When a national news network wanted me to stand outside the gates of the estate I was living in years ago, to say, "No, my husband did not agree to become Ferdinand and Imelda Marcos' lawyer," I said no. My husband asked me, "Don't you want to be on national TV?" I said no.

The interesting thing is that God begins to put His desires into your heart. I'm now excited about writing this book and excited about what God has in store for me. Colleen didn't miss the men or the bars; she was completely absorbed in the excitement of going around the world working for God. She had a sense of peace and contentment.

When Pastor JP Woods of Aspen gave up a six-figure a year job in the pharmaceutical industry to work in the ministry, he didn't think twice about the huge change in his economic status. Then one day, a friend he knew from the 'old days' asked him how it felt to be suddenly poor. He laughed and said he thought he was richer than he had ever been because he was rich in God's blessings. God changes the way you think about things.

Pastor Paul Perea and his wife Carol of the Assembly of God Church in Glenwood Springs are Hispanic Americans. Their families have been in the United States for many generations and they didn't have a 'Hispanic identity'. A few years after they became born again, Paul felt the Lord tell him to start a Spanish speaking charismatic church. Both Paul and Carol balked at this. Number one, they didn't speak

Spanish, and number two; they didn't want to minister to Hispanic immigrants they felt they couldn't relate to.

However, in obedience, they set upon the task of learning Spanish and quit their lucrative jobs in Grand Junction. Feeling that God was leading them to move to Glenwood Springs, they started a church with only two people. The first few months they would sometimes have as many as ten people attending their Bible study/prayer group. Most of the time however, they preached to just one couple. Within two and a half years, their little church of two has grown into a congregation of two hundred. Paul is now fluent in Spanish, with his wife, not far behind. They have both learned to appreciate their rich heritage and it has been an unparalleled blessing to lead so many to a close personal relationship with Christ. Their church is a spirit-filled place of miracles. People are delivered from drug addiction and alcoholism regularly. Healings and miracles are becoming commonplace. My housekeeper, Sylvia, attends their church. She told me that she believes the strength of their church lies in the fact that they have so many prayer groups all over the valley.

Isn't it interesting that instead of choosing someone who already spoke Spanish and was deeply committed to the immigrant population, God chose someone like Paul and Carol? It seems that God often picks unlikely people with major obstacles to do the job.

One of the best books on how God uses the most unlikely people in powerful ministries is Harvest, by Chuck Smith, the founder of the Calvary Churches. Chuck was at the forefront of the 'Jesus freak' movement in the early 70's. He was the pastor to the hippies. Ironically, Chuck was a super-straight pastor with a medical school background who never deviated from the middle. He was not a longhaired hippie himself who could relate to those that God wanted him to pastor. In fact, when God first called him as a minister to hippies in Southern California, I'm sure he felt somewhat uncomfortable. But when he reached out to the first hippie in love, the rewards were enormous.

Harvest is a marvelous collection of the life stories of many of the pastors in the Calvary Churches who lead congregations numbering in the thousands. From druggies, outlaw bikers, to one man who was 'addicted' to the killing fields of Vietnam, they run the entire gamut of sinners. Yet, when God called their names, they rose to meet the challenge through the intervention of people like Chuck Smith who reached out to them in love and became powerful pastors.

One of the most intriguing things I found about Chuck is that when he hears a story of a rebellious teenager on drugs, committing crimes and seemingly headed for hell, he often makes comments like, "I'll be curious to see where that young man is in ten years. The Lord must have a powerful purpose in his life."

Remember that things aren't always the way they seem. Both Moses and King David committed murder. The apostle Paul was involved in hunting down and killing Christians before being saved. Jacob was a liar who stole his brother's birthright and Samson was given over to his lusts. Its not what you've done but where your heart is right now that counts. God can and will use anybody.

A friend once agonized, "How can God even want to use me when I continue to sin over and over again?" I reminded her that the apostle Paul said, "We know that the law is spiritual; but I am unspiritual, sold as a slave to sin. I do not understand what I do. For what I want to do I do not do, but what I hate I do. And if I do what I do not want to do, I agree that the law is good. As it is, it is no longer I myself who do it, but it is sin living in me. I know that nothing good lives in me, that is, in my sinful nature. For I have the desire to do what is good, but I cannot carry it out. For what I do is not the good I want to do; no, the evil I do not want to do—this I keep on doing. Now if I do what I do not want to do, it is no longer I who do it, but it is sin living in me that does it.

"So I find this law at work. When I want to do good, evil is right there with me. For in my inner being I delight in God's law, but I see another law at work in the members of my body, waging war against the law of my mind and making me a prisoner of the law of sin at work within my members. What a wretched man I am! Who will rescue me from this body of death? Thanks be to God-through Jesus Christ our Lord!" (Romans 7:14-25,NIV) God uses us with all our weaknesses. He said to the apostle, Paul, "My grace is sufficient for you, for my power is made perfect in weakness" (2 Corinthians 12:9,NIV).

If God can use someone like me, He can use anyone. Only I know the dark places in my heart and the sin I've been in. Thank God I'm a new creation in Christ and God only see Christ's perfection in me. I don't have to stand before the throne on my own but clad in the righteousness of Jesus Christ. Everything good about me is from Him. It is not my goodness that people see, nor is it any of my other friends' goodness. What shines from our faces is the goodness of Christ. It is Jesus who has given us the beauty within that radiates from our soul. We reach out in love because He loves us.

Of course, there are those who hate us or think badly of us. Bless them. God tells us, "But I tell you who hear me: Love your enemies, do good to those who hate you, bless those who curse you, pray for those who mistreat you." I once drove past a sign on a church that read: "Be nice to your enemies. It will drive them crazy." Hate has nowhere to go when love is returned back.

The love of God enables us to be better people than we actually are. A friend of mine once told her new boyfriend, "Everything you love about me is from God. I wasn't this way before, God changed me." How fortunate we are that this life-changing gift is free for the asking. As Jesus pointed out in Matthew 9:12 (NIV): "It is not the healthy who need a doctor, but the sick. But go and learn what this means: 'I desire mercy, not sacrifice.' For I have not come to call the righteous, but sinners."

I am so grateful to the Lord for using a sinner like me. Trust Him and He will use you. Don't deny the power of God to transform you and use you in marvelous, miraculous ways. Remember its "not by power, nor by might, but by the Spirit of the Lord" alone that you can do anything. Allow God to channel His spirit within you to do, as Jesus says, "greater things than these".

I have found peace in doing God's will and my anxiety over my life has drained away. I truly believe that it was God who told me, "Write my book and I'll take care of everything else in your life." Interestingly, as I write this book, I have found that so much of what interested me before isn't as important as it used to be.

It may sound like superfluous nonsense to you, but here in Aspen it's easy to get caught up in the social whirl. However, it has become more important to me to be able to spend significant time with the Lord whether it's hiking or skiing alone. The parties, the clothes, and the jewelry do not glitter as brightly as they used to. Being invited to every party isn't important.

Where do your riches and desires lie? In the things of this world or in that which has eternal value?

God changes your desires and makes them consistent with His will. You don't miss the things of the world because God fills your time with things that matter in the eternal scheme of things. I cannot tell you the enormous contentment and joy I feel when someone tells me, "When you reached out to me, it changed my life. I saw Jesus in your life and it set me on the road to finding Him." What can be more fulfilling than that? Nothing makes you feel so good as helping another human being find some degree of peace in their lives.

God is so great and so good that He doesn't care where you've been or what you've done. We all have made mistakes and have done things we're not proud of. God chooses not to remember them if we ask Him to forgive us. All that matters is where we go from here.

Open yourself up to the Lord Jesus Christ and He will change your heart and your mind and give you the wonderful peace of knowing that everything is in His hands. Miracles happen because you are a child of God. Take your rightful place and trust that He will do what's best for you.

CHAPTER ELEVEN

SURRENDER

———— ❖ ————

Let us examine the subject of 'surrender' to the Lord. Surrendering ourselves to God entails much more than throwing our hands in the air and saying, "I give up!" The more difficult task is in giving up old habits and thought patterns that might have been the major contributor to the problem itself. We are often more comfortable with the problems we have lived with for so long than the great unknown. We've learned to live with the negativity we surround ourselves with, secretly fearing freedom from those 'demons' (or problems) in our lives that hold us in bondage.

It can affect our miracle in such a way that even after we receive our miracle, the denial of it can put us right back where we were before we started.

I was told the following story of a woman who had been wheelchair-bound for over fifty years. Happily married to her high school sweetheart the second time around, she still yearned to be able to walk again. She joined a prayer group that and one day, it was her turn for a miracle. She was told to get up and walk, not just across the marble floors but up and down the stairs. An important factor to consider is that in order to receive her healing, she had to get out of her wheelchair in faith and start walking. We often have to affirm the miracle by getting up and walking.

In faith, she got out of her wheelchair and within

minutes was almost running up and down the stairs in excitement. When her husband came to pick her up, his first reaction was, "What are you doing out of your wheelchair? Get back in."

The woman refused quietly and said, "I've been healed."

Despite the fact that the woman was standing right in front of her husband, having walked down to greet him, her husband argued, "No you haven't. Now just get back in the wheelchair so we can go home."

She was persuaded not to get in the wheelchair again, and they folded the wheelchair, putting it in the trunk of the car. Before the woman left, she was advised, "Don't ever get back in that wheelchair again. You've been healed."

A week later, the woman was back in the wheelchair. The truth of the matter was that, in a sense, she depended on the wheelchair to validate her existence and could only see herself as an invalid. She missed the attention the wheelchair gave her. Her husband played a key role in this woman losing her miracle. He had enjoyed taking care of her and now felt useless. They both could not surrender their need for attention; his need to 'mother' her and the insecurities that prompted them to hide behind the wheelchair.

You cannot receive, nor can you sustain a miracle if you cannot surrender your entire world of feelings. This is what often holds back our miracle. Although we ask, we inwardly fear receiving the miracle because of the changes it will bring in our lives. We don't know how we will feel in new circumstances and in our new skin because we have gotten so used to our circumstances and our illness.

The bottom line is, are you truly ready to surrender

yourself? Because a miracle will change your entire life, sometimes in unexpected ways. God doesn't always answer your prayers in the way you think he should. And sometimes, when He answers your prayers, it comes with additional circumstances that force changes into your life. Some of you may already know this in your own heart, and the fear of this, despite desperate pleading, may be stopping your own miracle.

When we pray for other people, it is important that we surrender them to God and place them on His altar. Do you want change in your children, your spouse, some other family member or friend? Are you ready to allow God to change them through your prayers no matter how much it will affect your life? We pray, "God change our children," not realizing that He may answer your prayers in a way that does not fit with your preconceived notions.

We all have hopes and dreams for our children. When we watch them, steeped in rebellion and sin, are we really able to release them to God, to work on their lives as He sees fit? When we say, "God change our children, bring them to salvation in Jesus Christ", have we completely released their future to God? Or do we want what we want and only what we want for them? Do we insist that upon their going to Harvard to become a lawyer? Are we able to trust God enough to release them to whatever God has in store for them? What if He, in His infinite wisdom, brings them to salvation and turns them into poor pastors to drug addicts in the ghettos? Or sends them to developing countries as missionaries? Or decides that they need to be construction workers rather than doctors? Can you surrender your children's entire lives to an omniscient God or do you still want to control your children because you think you know best?

I don't mean to say that God won't send your child to Harvard and that you shouldn't pray for that to happen. There's probably some of you out there who God has laid upon your heart to pray for your son or daughter to go to a specific school and take up a specific profession. I'm just pointing out a principle of surrender. Many parents I know have been led to simply surrender their children, in prayer, to the will of God.

At times, God takes a while to answer our prayers for our children because He needs to work on us first in order that we might learn how to totally surrender them to His will. Perhaps He needs to continue to work on them so that the seed will not fall on rocky soil. He is working the soil in order that real and lasting changes will be instituted.

Sadly, I know a woman who prayed for salvation for her spouse and after it came, the marriage broke up. Why? Because although her spouse changed, she could not release the bitterness and anger she continued to harbor and found herself unable to accept the miracle and was skeptical that he really had changed. In her mind, her husband was faking his acceptance of Christ. Perhaps, before we ask God to change someone else, we must totally release ourselves to Him and ask Him to change us first.

Miraculously, I have seen people change because the very people who were praying for them changed. My brother-in-law, Lloyd Horibe was raised Buddhist and sought God in different religions, not accepting or rejecting anything. Lloyd is very close to my brother Lincoln, who completely changed when he became born again. The drugs and the anger that had ruled his life so relentlessly disappeared and a new softness enveloped him. Slow to anger and accepting of every setback, God did an amazing work in his life and he now has an amazing peace that defies his circumstances. Knowing the way he used to be, this new peace and joy was a magnet to the agnostic Lloyd and he began to investigate Christ. Lloyd now says, "I became a Christian watching the incredible changes in Lincoln. I wanted the peace and joy he had."

Evelyn Christianson, a great writer of prayer books, wrote a book entitled, Lord, Change Me! Before we ask God to change anybody, ask Him first to change you. Sometimes that's all we need.

When you pray for a loved one, visualize that person bathed in the light of Jesus Christ. Picture the pure white light of Christ enveloping that person and ask for a spiritual, physical and emotional healing. The work to effectuate this prayer was done on the cross. Believe this and your loved one will receive a miracle through your faith.

Many parents came to Jesus and asked for healing for their children. This example demonstrates that it is valid to ask for a healing for someone else. Many Pentecostal Christians 'stand in the gap' and pray for unbelievers. Interestingly, healing is not just for believers. Healing can come to unbelievers through the faith of an intercessor.

I find prayers that change other people the most miraculous. It fascinates me to be witness to someone praying for a loved one and without saying anything to that person, watch that person change. I remember a pastor once saying, "You don't convert anyone, the Holy Spirit does the converting. Your job is to pray for that person."

For months my housekeeper Sylvia prayed diligently for

her husband to become born again. She didn't nag but she routinely asked him if he wanted to go to church with her every Sunday. Every Sunday he said no. Instead of preaching, she prayed. After three months of consistent prayer he suddenly surprised her by saying yes. Today he is an active member of their Spanish-speaking Assembly of God church participating in the music ministry.

There is a very fine line between surrendering the answer to the Lord and the double-mindedness that occurs when we pray, "thy will be done". Many pastors believe that in praying "thy will be done", we are praying amiss. Instead of ending the prayer with "thy will be done", we should instead say, "Get up and walk," affirming that which we desire. God desires healing, how can we believe He would want us to be sick? We throw doubt into the picture by saying, "thy will be done".

I want to point out that there is a difference between denying that you are sick and denying the fact that your sickness has the right to stay. There are schools of thought that believe you should deny the existence of any negativity in your life. That is not truth. The Spirit of God is the Spirit of Truth and cannot operate in a lie. The negativity or illness exists, we only deny the right of it to continue to stay and torment us. Come into agreement with God's words of healing in the Bible, and affirm our right to be healed and receive our miracle in all circumstances.

It is important to confirm in His word that what we are seeking is not contrary to His word. Then we should just go for it—praying affirmatively; "Thank you God for bringing this into my life." If we surrender ourselves and the people we pray for to God while seeking Him, then that which we desire is God's will. Believe it, trust it and go with it. I truly believe that the Lord loves us so much that He will not let us stagger around in uncertainty for very long if we are truly put Him first in our life. "Seek first his kingdom and His righteousness, and all these things will be given to you as well" (Matthew 6:33,NIV).

I know how difficult this is. I have staggered around in the wilderness for extended periods of time bogged down in the mire of uncertainty. I have asked God to make it clear to me and have felt even more confused. In my confusion, I became more and more self-absorbed. My problem became the focus of my entire life. It was not surprising that I was caught in the quicksand of my own creation. I had made the problem too big by giving it too much attention.

It is a principle in life that we give power to that which we focus our attention on. If we persist on focusing on the negative, we continually re-affirm its power in our lives. You must visualize and claim the positive. We are what we say and think. There is power in thoughts and words.

Brainwashing requires a constant diet of propaganda. Prisoners of war recount being forced to listen to a constant drone of anti-American, defeatist sentiment. This technique is not so different from the theory of subliminal perception that mesmerized people over ten years ago. Subliminal perception involved the use of innocuous, melodic tapes that whispered to your semi-conscious whatever it was that you wanted to happen in your life. Proponents touted it as the perfect way to lose weight, relieve stress and basically empower you to do anything you wanted to do. The message worked on your subconscious to create the reality in the flesh. You don't need tapes. You can empower yourself with

God's help in "speaking things that are not as if they were".

Put your mind and heart on Jesus. "Enter His gates with prayer and thanksgiving" and the focus will switch from you to the Lord. When you put God first, things will start to fall into place because everything is in the right order. God first before your problems. "Do not worry", the Lord says over and over again in the Bible. When we cease to worry, the focus shifts from you to the Lord. Peace and the ultimate answer come when we finally find that right balance.

Turn everything over to the Lord. Petition Him earnestly and consistently then begin to claim in faith that you have received your answer. Follow up by thanking God for your answer. Praise Him for answering your prayers in advance. This is a prayer of faith. Thanking God before you receive your answer is an act of faith. It is your statement that you know that God can do anything and it is reaffirming the fact that He loves you enough to do anything. Therein lies the power in prayer, praise and thanksgiving. Faith is manifested in these actions.

I want to give you one final example of surrender and the power that is released through prayer.

I knew a beautiful woman who seemed to lead a charmed life. Married to a very wealthy man, she lived in a beautiful mansion with park-like grounds. They had three children she adored and lavished with everything money could buy. Her husband was absolutely crazy about her and indulged her every whim, denying her nothing.

I was one of the few people who knew that her childhood and young adulthood were very sad. Abandoned by her mother and father at a very young age, she had been raised by an aunt who resented having to take her in. She had an unhappy first marriage and was working as a secretary when she met her wealthy husband. From then on, her life turned around. Until the day she found out she had cancer throughout her entire body.

The cancer was so pervasive that the doctors refused her any treatments, telling her she had less than a year to live. Her husband took her all over the country trying to find a cure. My friend was devastated as she watched her fairytale life crumble.

During this time, she didn't want to hear about God. God had abandoned her as a young child and she had no use for Him. All she wanted was a medical miracle. If anything, she was angry with God and chose not to believe in a God who would do this to her.

Yet God was working in her life, softening her heart, showing her His love. She wrote to me saying that she woke up one day and suddenly 'got it'. She felt bathed in the love of Christ Jesus. A great peace settled over her and she knew that no matter what happened, everything was going to be all right. All her anxiety washed away and she began to cry tears of joy because she knew that Jesus was with her and He was not going to let her go through this alone.

The Lord gave my friend five extra years and she was able to see her children into their teen years and college. In His great mercy, He gave her the impossible, more time.

Did my friend receive her miracle? Absolutely. But she died, some of you will say. May I say this, our miracle doesn't always come the way we want or expect, but it always comes. There are some things that are just between you and God. There are many things that are beyond our ability to comprehend.

I am reminded of a story I was told when I first became a Christian by one of my best friends in Hawaii, Lucinda. My next door neighbor for years, Lucinda literally 'prayed me into the kingdom'. Lucinda told me of a man in her Bible study class who gave this amazing description of life. He said that life was like a piece of needlepoint. On one side is a chaotic mess. That's the side we look at our life from. However, when you turn the needlepoint over, you see that the chaotic mess forms a beautiful picture. That's the side God sees our lives from.

That is what the apostle Paul meant when he said in his letter to the Corinthians, "for now I see through a glass darkly...but then, shall I see face to face". We will never understand everything until we enter God's kingdom. I suspect that when we do, we will see that God answered every prayer and gave us our miracles.

This is not a rationalization. My friend who died of cancer received peace and tranquility when she accepted Jesus as her savior. In His infinite kindness, God enabled her, to see her youngest child into high school. A devoted mother, the desire of her heart was for her children, rather than herself. That morning she woke up and wrote to me, God gave her the peace of knowing she would be fine, no matter what.

God is the great comforter who offers you peace in every circumstance and that is the greatest miracle of all.

CHAPTER TWELVE

KEYS TO THE KINGDOM

❖

You have just received the Keys to the Kingdom. As Jesus told the apostle Peter before the crucifixion, "I will give you the keys of the kingdom of heaven; whatever you bind on earth will be bound in heaven, and whatever you loose on earth will be loosed in heaven" (Matthew 16:19,NIV). Prayer is the most powerful, effectual tool we have. It is our 'telephone' to God. Isn't it glorious that we are able to reach the Almighty by just entering into prayer? What a privilege to be able to enter the throne room of the King of Kings with our prayers and petitions any time we want. Yet most of us fail to take advantage of this enormous privilege.

Where are your priorities? If your priority is God, it means you commune with Him daily. While you walk, shower, jog or work in the kitchen, you can spend time with the Lord. A favorite time for many people is driving to work. If you're stuck in that traffic jam anyway, you might as well have a heart to heart with the King of Kings.

Prayer will calm your spirit and infuse you with light and hope. Studies show that prayer will lower your blood pressure and make you optimistic and peaceful in every circumstance.

"Is any one of you in trouble? He should pray. Is anyone happy? Let him sing songs of praise. Is any one of you sick?

He should call the elders of the church to pray over him and anoint him with oil in the name of the Lord. And the prayer offered in faith will make the sick person well; the Lord will raise him up. If he has sinned, he will be forgiven. Therefore, confess your sins to each other and pray for each other so that you may be healed. The prayer of a righteous man is powerful and effective.

"Elijah was a man just like us. He prayed earnestly that it would not rain and it did not rain on the land for three and a half years. Again he prayed and the heavens gave rain, and the earth produced its crops" (James 5:13-18,NIV).

Jesus said, "Nothing shall be impossible for Him that believes."

I want to emphasize to you that Christianity is a positive message of love and hope. I repeat, the Bible says, "Therefore, there is now no condemnation for those who are in Christ Jesus" (Romans 8:1,NIV).

I was at a ladies luncheon in Aspen recently and two friends of mine were extolling the "Forum", the new, recycled version of Werner Erhardt's movement in the 70's called EST. One of them commented, "The thing I don't like about Christianity is that it's all about feeling guilty. It's so negative."

I pointed out that Christianity is the exact opposite of that. I submit people and religion have often subverted the true nature and message of our Lord Jesus Christ. The message is optimistic, life-affirming and loving. "God is love. Whoever lives in love lives in God, and God in him. In this way, love is made complete among us so that we will have confidence on the Day of Judgment, because in this world we are like Him. There is no fear in love. But perfect love drives out fear, because fear has to do with punishment. The one who fears is not made perfect in love.

"We love because He first loved us. If anyone says, 'I love God,' yet hates his brother, he is a liar. For anyone who does not love his brother, whom he has seen, cannot love God, whom he has not seen. And He has given us this command. Whoever loves God must also love his brother" (1John 4:16-21,NIV).

If you would just take the time to read God's word, you will find it a fascinating account of men and women whose lives were fraught with the anxieties and frailties of the world. They overcame enormous obstacles through faith, that which they could not conquer on their own. There were no super-humans, with the exception of Samson, only painfully ordinary people who God raised up despite their misgivings and doubts, to do wondrous things.

When the Lord Jesus Christ walked the earth, He did not choose the 'holy' or the 'righteous,' much to their chagrin. As He said, "The righteous think they're righteous enough". Jesus came for the sinners. I love the banner that hangs atop Heritage Christian Center in Denver that announces boldly for anyone within a couple of blocks away to see, "SINNERS WELCOME". In speaking of them, Jesus said, "He who is forgiven much, loves much".

God sees in us that which the human eye cannot see. He sees our spirit and that which we have the potential to become through His mercy and grace. That is why we can do anything in Christ Jesus. We are more than a conqueror in Christ for our flesh is but a poor shadow of what we really are. Our flesh is weak and fraught with problems and insecurities, but our spirit is beautiful to the Lord. Our spirit is encapsulated in the light of His love that is made perfect through Christ Jesus. Strip away the things of the world and we are Christ-like, not through our efforts or goodness, but through Him who makes us perfect. In us is the perfection of Christ Jesus if we tap into the power by asking, seeking and knocking. That action is our responsibility. We make the choice of seeking Jesus in whom all perfection is made available to us.

Jesus is sufficient for all of our needs and glory. Look for Him who makes us perfect. We enter the throne room through His cleansing and righteousness. As perfect human beings in Christ, we can ask anything, having the assurance that He will answer our prayers. We wear His glory when we accept his gift of salvation. Every time you fall and sin, get back under the blood so you can get back into the throne room.

Jesus will always take you back and show you a way out of impossible situations. The Lord showed me this truth quite graphically during a period in which I had backslidden and was grappling with my emotions. For two weeks I had prayed arid, 'canned' prayers as I pursued 'my way'. Have you ever noticed that when you are in 'sin' or insistent upon doing things your way that your prayer life suffers? Your spirit knows what your flesh is afraid of facing. We know that the spirit of the Lord speaks to us during prayer, therefore we don't seek God when we're afraid of the answer. However, no matter how far away we run, "there is no mountain high enough", as the song goes. God will bring us back.

God brought me back by locking me in a bathroom with no windows. I had just moved into a new house with no steam shower and so I decided to go back to my old house for a steam. The house was vacant and on the market, so I locked the bathroom door just in case the Realtors came by with clients. After my shower, I unlocked the door and tried to turn the doorknob. To my horror, I discovered that the doorknob was broken. Frantically I spun the useless doorknob and began to pray. As I prayed, I looked around for something in the bathroom to pry the hinges off the door or unscrew the knob. I couldn't find anything and began to panic. Because it was off-season in Aspen, I knew that it was possible that no one would show the house for weeks. No one knew where I was and every house in my neighborhood was situated on one-acre lots; which meant that no one would hear me if I screamed. Most of my neighbors were second homeowners and their houses were presently vacant. I began to envision starving to death in a locked bathroom.

I told myself to calm down. I stopped what I was doing and prayed, "God, you're the only one who can help me. I can't even help myself. Please get me out of here." Taking a deep breath, I put my hand out and grabbed the doorknob. The door literally sprang open. I began to praise God and thank Him for setting me free.

I knew then that God was trying to tell me something. I had avoided Him for two weeks and knew that this was His way of getting my attention. I had a feeling I knew what God was trying to tell me, but I wanted confirmation. The next morning, I woke up at 4am. Unable to go back to sleep, I picked up my Bible and opened it at random to Daniel 6:16-22 (NIV). "So the king (Nebuchadnezzar) gave the order, and they brought Daniel and threw him into the lions' den. The king said to Daniel, "May your God, whom you serve continually, rescue you!"

"A stone was brought and placed over the mouth of the den, and the king sealed it with his own signet ring and with the rings of his nobles, so that Daniel's situation might not be changed...he (Nebuchadnezzar) called to Daniel..."Daniel, servant of the living god, has your God, whom you serve continually, been able to rescue you from the lions?"

"Daniel answered, '...My God sent his angel, and he shut the mouths of the lions....'"

"Being like Gideon who wanted "just one more sign," I asked God to show me one more passage so I would know I didn't just come upon that story by accident. I closed the Bible and opened it to Acts 12:5-11 (NIV). "So Peter was kept in prison, but the church was earnestly praying to God for him.

"The night before Herod was to bring him to trial, Peter was sleeping between two soldiers, bound with two chains, and sentries stood guard at the entrance. Suddenly an angel of the Lord appeared and a light shone in the cell. He struck Peter on the side and woke him up. "Quick, get up!" he said and the chains fell off Peter's wrists.

"...Then Peter came to himself and said, "Now I know without a doubt that the Lord sent his angel and rescued me from Herod's clutches and from everything the Jewish people were anticipating."'"

Like Gideon, God gave me three signs to tell me that I was imprisoned by my emotions. However, if I repented and asked Him to help me, He would show me the way out of the prison I had put myself in. I knew that if I continued on the same path, I would eventually find myself in the lions' den.

I cried because I had always known the answer. That was why my prayer life had been so lukewarm. I didn't want to do what I knew I had to do. However, I knew that if I didn't, the happiness I so desperately sought would never be mine. I would never be at peace as long as I eluded God and His will in my life.

I did what God asked of me and renewed my commitment to put Him first in my life. Miraculously, a great peace settled over me and the pain I thought I would feel never came. When we are in God's will, He provides a way out of the pain and heartache we often create for ourselves. Another key important factor was that several people were praying for me.

Ask of Him everything that is in your heart. He is so merciful and kind that He provides you with a way out of any mess you may find yourself in. You may have put yourself in prison, but God will deliver you from the chains that bind you. He answers each and every prayer in a way that is best for you. Trust His answer. Trust Him. He knows what's best for you even if you can't see how His answer could possibly be good for you at the time. After all, God knows all your yesterdays, is aware of today and will control all of your tomorrow's, if you allow it. Do you trust God with the answer or do you just want what you want-NO MATTER WHAT?

I have had to learn to release my tomorrow's to God while writing this book. I know very well that 'giving it to the Lord' sounds easy, but isn't. We all want what we want. We all think we know what's best for us. If we had our way, we would mess up our lives continually. Things aren't always what they seem. Beautiful fruit may be bitter inside.

The storms of life may simply be what God is using to blow blessings your way.

I have learned to appreciate my wilderness experiences because I know the Promised Land is just a prayer away. Pastor Leonard exhorts, "After the pain, comes the promise." Athletes and fitness freaks often say, "No pain, no gain." In order to build and tone your muscles, you have to take your body to its limits. We know our body is improving when we feel the pain from a workout the next day.

It is the rain that brings beautiful flowers. When it rains in your life, praise God because beautiful flowers are about to grow in your arid soil. One of my friends inspired me with this clever idea on changing a negative into a positive. "I try to think of the dark cloud that's been following me as God's shadow hovering protectively over me."

"Yea, though I walk through the valley of the shadow of death, I will fear no evil, for thou art with me; thy rod and thy staff, they comfort me...surely goodness and mercy will follow me all the days of my life, and I will dwell in the house of the Lord forever". (Psalm 23, NKJV).

God loves you and me. Blessed is the name of the Lord. Blessed is Elohim Adonai who answers my prayers. Because of this glorious fact, we are free to experience our lives in Christ Jesus without fear or confusion. Our answer is on the way the minute our prayer leaves our lips. God is never too late. And God is all love and forgiveness.

Kenneth Copeland, in Love Never Fails poses an interesting assertion. In wondering why Jesus never retaliated, he realized Jesus fought back with love. Compassion and love always defeats hatred.

The message of Jesus Christ has endured for thousands

of years. Therefore, His death on the cross was a victory and His resurrection a promise of eternal life to mankind. This compelling gift of eternal life is a free gift that has never changed. God promises to forgive us if we simply accept the Lord Jesus Christ as our Savior who died for our sins.

How complete is His forgiveness? One of the most cold-blooded serial killers that ever lived was Ted Bundy. It has been said that in his last days, Ted Bundy made a confession for Christ and was born again. If he did, then he is in heaven. As difficult as it may be for some people to accept this, to deny that God did so is to deny the Bible.

God's forgiveness and love is beyond our human ability to understand. Quit trying to figure out God and accept in faith that as God, He is not like us nor will He ever be. Thank goodness that He loves us and forgives us no matter what we have done. Besides, we have so much to ask of God, we really don't have the time to worry about whether or not God has forgiven serial killers. On top of that, doesn't it make you better able to totally grasp the concept of your own forgiveness by a God who is so compassionate that He is able to forgive someone like Ted Bundy? Now do you accept your own forgiveness?

Remember that in His time, the ruling body, the Pharisees, hated Jesus because, among other things, He hung out with sinners like prostitutes and thieves. He chose as apostles people who were very low on the social scale, like simple fishermen. Jesus was definitely not an elitist.

That is why He chose me to write this book. An unknown sinner who has lived a spectacularly dysfunctional life and has truly seen life, as Joni Mitchell sang, "from both sides now". He chose you or you wouldn't be reading this book.

Praise God that you have been handpicked to be a part of His kingdom. As Jesus said, "You did not choose me but I chose you to go and bear fruit—fruit that will last. Then the Father will give you whatever you ask in my name" (John 15:16,NIV).

As His chosen one, how can you doubt that He has a miracle just waiting for you? All you have to do is ask and believe with all your heart that the God of miracles wants to do a miracle for you.

As Paul argues in the eighth chapter in the book of Romans (NIV): "If God is for us, who can be against us? He who did not spare His own Son, but gave Him up for us all—how will he not also, along with Him, graciously give us all things? Who will bring any charge against those whom God has chosen? It is God who justifies. Who is He that condemns? Christ Jesus, who died—more than that, who was raised to life—is at the right hand of God and is also interceding for us. Who shall separate us from the love of Christ? Shall trouble or hardship or persecution or famine or nakedness or danger or sword? As it is written:

"For your sake we face death all day long;

we are considered as sheep to be slaughtered."

"No, in all these things we are more than conquerors through Him who loved us. For I am convinced that neither death nor life, neither angels nor demons, neither the present nor the future, nor any powers, neither height nor depth, nor anything else in all creation, will be able to separate us from the love of God that is in Christ Jesus our Lord".

If nothing can separate us from the love of Christ Jesus then how can we doubt that He wants to do a miracle for us in this life? Therefore, "rejoice in our sufferings, because we know that suffering produces perseverance; character; and character, hope. And hope does not disappoint us, because God has poured out His love into our hearts by the Holy Spirit, whom He has given us" (Romans 5:3-5,NIV).

Through the indwelling of the Holy Spirit, He empowers us to do 'all things' if we just believe. That is 'God within us'. We are not gods, as the New-Agers would have us believe. This is one of the biggest lies of the devil, the original sin that Eve fell into. The devil told Eve through the serpent, "For God knows that when you eat of it (the forbidden fruit) your eyes will be opened, and you will be like God..." (Genesis 3:5,NIV) From that time forward, man, as well as the devil, has tried to take God's place.

The wonderful truth is that we have always had the ability to tap into God's power and find God within us. Don't let yourself be defeated by your circumstances. Stand up and take your rightful place as a child of the King. Tap into the mighty power of God through the Holy Spirit who lies dormant within, just waiting for you to knock and open that door. You don't have to walk in defeat and darkness any longer. Jesus told you that you would be able to do 'greater things' because He stands in the throne room personally interceding for you. He is your attorney in the Holy of Holies. Yes, the devil is the prosecutor, but do you believe that there is no power stronger than that of Christ Jesus? How can you lose when you've got someone on your side who has never lost a case?

Trust in the Lord to work everything out for your good. No matter what storm you are in, He is in the boat with you. If you should be thrown into the fire, He's there too. Your miracle is right around the corner because the power of God lies within. Call upon Him through the Lord Jesus Christ and He will make all things possible. You don't have to be a slave to worry, frustration, bitterness and defeat any longer. "You are more than a conqueror in Christ Jesus."

God said, "For I know the plans I have for you, plans to give you hope and a future. Then you will call upon me and come and pray to me, and I will listen to you. You will seek me and find me when you seek me with all your heart. I will be found by you,' declares the Lord...." (Jeremiah 29:11-14,NIV).

"For this reason I kneel before the Father, from whom His whole family in heaven and on earth derives its name. I pray that out of His glorious riches He may strengthen you with power through His Spirit in your inner being, so that Christ may dwell in your hearts through faith. And I pray that you, being rooted and established in love, may have power, together with all the saints, to grasp how wide and long and high and deep is the love of Christ, and to know this love that surpasses knowledge-that you may be filled to the measure of all the fullness of God.

"Now to Him who is able to do immeasurably more than all we ask or imagine, according to His power that is at work within us, to him be glory in the church and in Christ Jesus throughout all generations, forever and ever! Amen" (Ephesians 3:14-21,NIV).

Thank you, Abba (Father in Hebrew), for your mercy and your grace. Thank you, Jesus, for dying for my sins. Thank you for the cross and the blood of Jesus by which I am justified and made righteous. Thank you, Holy Spirit, for your presence in my life that makes all things possible for anyone who just believes. Thank you for the miracles that you ordered to be manifested in my life yesterday, today and tomorrow. I thank you and praise you for this book that was written through the Holy Spirit as a testimony on faith and a teaching tool so that those who are in pain can learn how to tap into the miracles you want to do for them. Thank you for your Word that has survived through the ages and is still, to this day, your promise to us. I know that you will answer each and every prayer in a miraculous way. I stand upon your promise to give me the desires of my heart if I continue to praise, worship, and trust in you. I know that "they that wait upon the Lord shall renew their strength: they shall mount up with the wings of eagles; they shall run, and not be weary; they shall walk, and not faint." (Isaiah 40:31, King James). No matter how long it takes, I will never give up, but continue to put all my hope and trust in you. I know that my answer is on the way. Lord, grant me patience, for I know that your timing is perfect. Most of all, I praise you for wrapping everyone who loves you in the cocoon of your perfect, agape love and granting them eternal life in your kingdom. Thank you for your saving grace. In Jesus' name I pray, Amen.